CW00691234

The Quilt

BY

DAVID AND DENNIS MCINTYRE

The Quilt

Copyright © 2022 by David P. McIntyre and Dennis A. McIntyre

All rights reserved. No part of this book may be used or reproduced by any means, graphic, electronic, or mechanical, including photocopying, recording, taping or by any information storage retrieval system without the written permission of the publisher except in the case of brief quotations embodied in critical articles and reviews.

Bennett books may be ordered through booksellers or by contacting:

Bennett Media and Marketing
1603 Capitol Ave., Suite 310 A233
Cheyenne, WY 82001
www.thebennettmediaandmarketing.com
Phone: 1-307-202-9292

Because of the dynamic nature of the Internet, any web addresses or links contained in this book may have changed since publication and may no longer be valid. The views expressed in this work are solely those of the author and do not necessarily reflect the views of the publisher, and the publisher hereby disclaims any responsibility for them.

Any people depicted in stock imagery provided by Shutterstock are models, and such images are being used for illustrative purposes only.

Certain stock imagery © Shutterstock

ISBN: 978-1-957114-20-0 (hardcover)
ISBN: 978-1-957114-18-7 (softcover)
ISBN: 978-1-957114-19-4 (eBook)

Printed in the United States of America

TABLE OF CONTENTS

DAVID AND DENNIS MCINTYRE

CHAPTER 1:
BEGINNINGS

Laverne was the third child of Rex and Verna Mae (Allen) McIntyre. Rex was born in 1886 and Verna in 1887. They had four children: Roy Wesley born in 1907, Walter Allen born in 1909, Laverne Stewart born June 4th, 1911, and Effie May born in 1912. Laverne was born in Galeton, Pennsylvania. It was a small town in north central Pennsylvania just across the New York/Pennsylvania border. At that time, the population was at its peak with about 4 thousand residents. The town was a major supplier of lumber and leather and was known for logging camps and sawmills. The town boasted that it had the largest 3 blade sawmill producing hemlock lumber in the country. Logging and chemical plants and other factories related to the lumber industry provided most of the jobs in the area. Rex probably worked as a lumberjack at that time.

The 20th century America saw a great many changes. It was a century of wars, scientific advances, innovation, urbanization, social changes and much more. By the time Laverne was 3 years old, World War I had broken out in Europe. Largely it was a war between France, Russia, and Great Britain against Germany, Austria-Hungary, and Italy. It was fought in trenches on two fronts in France and Russia. America initially was not much interested in the war. It was just something that was happening over in Europe but did not affect Americans.

Indirectly it did. The need for war related supplies: munitions, equipment, better weapons, etc. were needed in large quantities. Industries supplying these things grew tremendously. Rochester, New York experienced a war boom as Kodak supplied aerial camera equipment. Stromberg-Carlson supplied telephone and radio equipment. Gleason supplied tools, gears, and castings. Bausch and Lomb supplied optical glass needed in all kinds of equipment as well as a host of other manufacturers supplying munitions.

America was initially neutral on the war. The sinking of the liner Lusitania on May 7, 1915 changed America's mind. People started to really dislike the Germans. America finally declared war on Germany in April 1917. By the time the war ended in 1918, the total stats were staggering. The world estimates were 40 million casualties: roughly 20 million deaths from battle or disease and 20 million wounded. Even though the United States stayed out of the war until the last year, 116,000 Americans were killed or wounded[1]. The war finally ended with the Treaty of Versailles and the League of Nations was formed largely to prevent such future devastating conflicts. World War I was supposed to be the war to end all wars.

Laverne, of course being only 7 at wars end, was totally oblivious to the events but his family was certainly affected. Manufacturing plants grew in many cities which drew a great many from the rural areas into cities to find jobs. The Galeton area was decimated by the logging industry. Ten years after Laverne was born, the town had lost over 26 percent of its population. The waning of the logging industry in Galeton and the need for more workers in Rochester may well have prompted Rex and Verna to move the family to that city. There was a picture with Rex and 3 other men representing 4 generations at that time. Rex apparently was one of those tough exterior Irishman who may have liked to drink. Verna, his wife, and Laverne's mother loved him dearly and always spoke well of her Rex.

People were optimistic with the ending of World War I. The war to end all wars was done and the League of Nations was created to ensure there would

---

1 Wikipedia

be no future wars. Industry was growing. The job market was good. People were earning money and spending it. New inventions made life easier. The vacuum cleaner was invented in 1901, the electric washing machine in 1907, neon lamps in 1910. By 1908 Henry Ford was producing the Model T on an assembly line. There were a host of other things too. People had more time for leisure activities. The 1920's began with a roar.

The twenties also brought a host of present and future problems. The movement of people from the farms to the cities left the farms desperate for workers. African Americans migrated from the South to the Northern cities and ended up clustered in all black neighborhoods. Meanwhile, America was inundated with immigrants from war-torn countries in Europe and they too ended up clustered in their own neighborhoods. The tension between those neighborhoods would increase inevitably leading to riots and even murders. Conflicts sprang up between city and small-town residents, Protestants and Catholics, blacks, and whites. Communism in Russia and Eastern Europe carried over to the United States and brought a widespread anti-immigrant hysteria. The youth, as is always the case, rebelled against parental authority and developed their own slang, listened to their own music, and danced the Charleston. It was an era of the big bands. There was also a desire for alcohol consumption which the older population tried to curtail with prohibition. That didn't work. The liquor establishments went underground in Speakeasies run by organized crime. The crime boss, Al Capone, was reported to have 1000 gunman and half of the Chicago police department on his payroll. In 1929, he was reported to have killed 7 of his competitors in the Saint Valentine's day massacre.

There were also more positive things as well. The first radio station started in 1920. By 1923, there were over 500 and by the end of the decade, there were radios in 12 million homes. The Model T Ford gave people especially the young a sense of freedom. You could buy one in 1924 for $260 and by 1929, there was one car for every 5 Americans. The collective wealth of the nation about doubled in the decade. It was also the golden age of Hollywood.

Warner Brothers, RKO, FOX, MGM, and Paramount dominated. People went to see Carlie Chaplin, the Marx Brothers, and Tallulah Bankhead. Films also provided a lot of news coverage. It began with newsreel shorts about the war effort during World War I.

The McIntyre family did OK during the early 1920's but then things began to change. Rex loved his cigars. That probably contributed to his demise. He developed throat cancer and died in 1928 at age 42. His decline and subsequent death was devastating to the family. The major bread winner was gone, and Verna had to find support for the family. The boys had to help. Roy would have been about 21, Walt about 19, Laverne about 17 and Effie was 16. Everybody had to work and pool their incomes to keep the family going. Records indicate that Laverne made it into high school, but he claimed that he only finished the 8th grade. Perhaps the pending loss of his father contributed to his dropping out of school. Another event also had a major impact on the family's financial position. The stock market crashed in 1929 and ushered in the depression of the 1930's. While statistics tell us only about 16 percent of the American people had money in the stock market the ripple effect of that crash affected nearly everyone in the country. Half the banks failed. At the lowest point during that time, the unemployment rate was about 25 percent. The 1930's saw the great dust bowl where a million acres of farmland in the great plains become worthless due to drought and over farming. It had a devastating effect on prices and availability of food. It was an exceedingly difficult time. Crime was rampant. 1934 saw three famous criminals killed: John Dillinger on July 22 and later that year after a crime spree Bonnie and Clyde. Still, people went to the movies to escape their circumstances for a while. Hollywood cranked out some of the best loved movies of all times during the depression years. The following is a partial list:

Snow White and the Seven Dwarfs
Mr. Smith Goes to Washington
Gone With the Wind
Citizen Kane

The Wizard of Oz

Laverne did not have a college education, but he was good with his hands. He became a machinist helper and worked for Rochester Novelty Works. He also liked to play bridge as did his older brother Roy. Somewhere along the line, he met his future wife, Rae Diane Wyland.

Rae was born on December 19, 1914. She had a brother and later they were orphaned. She attended East High School in Rochester and was a very gifted student. Her yearbook described her as "a brilliant Rae of knowledge". In 1932 she attended the University of Rochester and later graduated in 1936 with a degree in mathematics. That was quite an accomplishment. The U. of R. was already established as a leading university in math and science.

Rae then began to work as an optical designer for Kodak in Rochester New York. She had gone onto college right out of high school, on a special program for orphans. She was just at age 21 The census in 1940 indicated that she was working there at that time. She also was elected to membership in the American Mathematical Society December 27, 1942. The June 29, 1943 Kodakery, Kodak's employee newspaper, published a picture of Rae with 3 gentlemen who were being installed as Hawk-eye Camera Club officers. She was also nominated for secretary in that same club the following year as well (a picture appeared in the June 12, 1944 Kodakery).

To be Installed—Recently elected to head the Hawk-Eye Camera Club during the coming year, the four officers above will be installed at the ceremonies opening the club's new darkrooms within the next few weeks. From left, Milt Richardson, Rae Wyland, Sherm Montgomery and Lou Parker.

Camera Club Plans Loan Print Shows

Air Warfare in World War I Child's Play, Inspector Says

Plans for a traveling print show

She also was a bridge player. There was a reference in the February 8, 1944, Kodakery in which her future brother and sister in law, Mr. and Mrs. Roy McIntyre, were mentioned as winning second place in the Maplewood WMCA bridge tournament. The referenced specified that they were friends of Rae D. Wyland. Laverne was an avid bridge player and that may have been how they met. Did Laverne's oldest brother, Roy, and his wife introduce him to Rae? Did that mutual interest lead to a love connection? Laverne was a quiet man and did not share much about how he and Rae met. They did know each other before Laverne went off to war. Rae did well. She along with fellow scientist Fred E. Altman applied for a patent for a plastic objective lens in March 1943. They received the patent in November 1947 and that lens design may well have been instrumental in the development of some of Kodak's camera products.

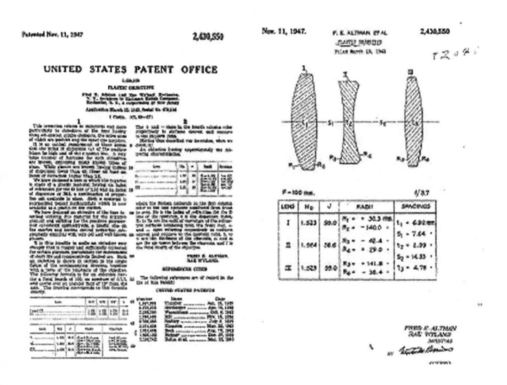

Rae Wyland

Verna Mae and Rae

CHAPTER 2:
THE CONFLICT

T he end of World War I and the Versailles Treaty left Germany defeated and humiliated. Inflation and political unrest were rampant. The German territory had been cut up and given over to other nations or new nations were formed such as Czechoslovakia, Austria, and Hungary. Germany was not allowed a navy or air force and only a skeleton army. The country was

bankrupt, plagued by unemployment and large segments of the population were under foreign rule. In the middle of this turmoil arose a National Socialist Party leader by the name of Adolf Hitler. He promised the people that he would restore the fatherland and recover the territories lost to give everyone more Lebensraum ("living space"). He also promised jobs and to get Germany back to its former glory. He struck a chord with the German people and they voted him in as Chancellor of the Third Reich in 1933.

Hitler was no savior. He was a deceiving, lying demagogue with a satanic agenda right from the start. He even published his views in Mein Kampf in 1925. It was a poorly written hodgepodge of his views on race, government, and the "Aryan" destiny. The following are some examples taken right from his book[2].

> "... Terror at the place of employment, in the factory, in the meeting hall and on occasion of mass demonstrations will always be successful, unless opposed by equal terror."

> "The receptivity of the great masses is very limited."

> "No boy and no girl must leave school without having been led to an ultimate realization of the necessity and essence of blood purity."

> "Bear in mind the devastation which Jewish bastardization visits on our nation each day, and consider that this blood poisoning can be removed from our national only after centuries, if at all... This contamination of our blood, blindly ignored by hundreds of thousands of our people, is carried on systematically by the Jew today. Systematically these black parasites of the nation defile our inexperienced young blond girls..."

---

2 "Reader's Digest Illustrated Story of World War II", American Reader's Digest association, Inc. 1969, pp 89-90

Hitler was driven. He was a master at manipulating the crowds, at trickery and deceit. He, very quickly, consolidated his power. He deceived the legislature into giving him "temporary" power which soon turned into total power. He destroyed the power of labor and forbade strikes, bound farmers to the land, seized control of churches, eliminated rival political parties, and turned the press into his personal propaganda arm. He did all of it with the blessing of the people because he gave them jobs. He talked openly of peace with all the surrounding nations while secretly preparing for war. In seven years, Germany was poised to dominate the entire world. He did it all right under the noses of all the foreign powers.

Once Germany's military might became strong enough, Hitler then set out to systematically add territory. Publicly he talked peace to the other nations, while through deception, manipulation, staged events, and outright lies, he implemented his plan. He first took advantage of the world's focus on Mussolini in Italy to reoccupy the Rhineland in 1936. The French could have easily stopped him; they had the military superiority over the German forces, but they did not. Had they done so, maybe they would have prevented World War II. The Rhineland fell. The League of Nations proved totally impotent to stop it. Hitler's gamble cemented his power and popularity. The Soviet Union,

Poland, Czechoslovakia, Rumania, and Yugoslavia now realized their ally, France was not going to assist them should Germany turn on them.

The next country to fall was Hitler's birthplace, Austria, in 1938. He harassed the Austrian Chancellor into signing an ultimatum and then proceeded with an election by the Austrian populace. The vote was 99 % yes, with the Nazi election committee watching how everyone voted. It was a brave Austrian who voted no. With Austria annexed, Hitler turned his attention to Czechoslovakia. The Czechs mobilized and Great Britain, France, and The Soviet Union displayed more backbone against the German bullies' threat. Hitler lied and said that Germany had no intentions on Czechoslovakia while at the same time inciting the German population in that country to riot. The riot gave him the pretext to move in. Some of Hitler's generals warned that a war with Great Britain, France, and the Soviet Union would mean the defeat of Germany. Hitler sensed that England and France would do almost anything to avoid war, so he ordered the army to move in in October 1938 and by March 1939 the country was under German control.

Germany 1939

Hitler now set his sights on Poland. He secretly paved the way with a non-aggression pact with the Soviet Union and he hoped that the attitude of appeasement by England and France would continue. He concocted a plan to have German SS forces attack a German radio station in Poland, dressed in Polish army uniforms, so that he could tell everyone that the Poles had attacked first. He sent the German army in, supposedly in response on September 1, 1939. The Soviet Union also attacked Poland intending to grab some of the territory for themselves. The master liar, bully, deceiver was at it again. This time, however, England, France declared war on Germany on September 3, 1939. World War II began. Germany aligned with Mussolini in Italy along with the territories to form the Axis powers against the Allied powers. Germany also had a secret pact with Japan that if the United States entered the war, Germany would declare war on the US.

Start WW II 1939 Attack on Poland
Axis - Germany,Italy
Allies - Great Britain, France

Hitler was not finished; he wanted world conquest. He next set his sights on Denmark and Norway to gain better access to the open ocean and protect Germany's source of desperately needed iron ore from Sweden. On April 9, 1940, he demanded that both countries accept instantly and without resistance protection from the Third Reich. Denmark could not defend itself, and capitulated. Norway resisted. The Southern part of the country was overrun quickly. The northern part with the help of the British held out for a while. Eventually the country fell, and Hitler now had his ocean access and new bases to use in an attack on Great Britain. He also gained access to valuable iron ore needed for his war effort. German losses were heavy, however, losing 10 out of 29 destroyers, 3 of 8 cruisers, 2 battle cruisers and a pocket battleship That meant that Hitler did not have the naval power to try to invade England.

He now turned his attention to Belgium and the Netherlands "to safeguard their neutrality against an imminent attack by the Anglo-French armies"[3]. His war machine continued the blitzkrieg (lightning war) into those countries on May 10, 1940. The Germany army pushed through the Ardennes and soundly defeated the French and the British. It is interesting that the same area later was the location of another push by the German army that was repulsed by the Allied forces and marked the beginning of the end for the Third Reich. That battle was known as the Battle of the Bulge. The Dutch surrendered to Germany on May 14, 1940. The Belgians surrendered on May 28, 1940. The British retreated to Dunkirk beach. For some reason Hitler stopped his army in sight of Dunkirk, perhaps believing the British would not be able to get off the beach. He was wrong. The resilient British people sent small boats across the

3 Ibid. "Reader's Digest Illustrated Story of World War II", p.73.

channel and rescued over 300,000 soldiers under the noses of the Germans[4]. It was one of the heroic stories of World War II.

Hitler now went after France. He sent a massive assault into the northern part of France while his supposed ally, Mussolini attacked the southern part. Paris was overrun by June 14. The French Premier Reynard resigned and was replaced by Marshal Henri Philippi Petain who asked for an armistice. The French finally capitulated on June 22, 1940. To sweeten his revenge on the French, Hitler held the ceremony on the very spot that 22 years earlier Germany had been humbled and forced to sign an armistice to end World War I. Once the armistice was signed, Phillippe Petain was made the authoritarian leader in France and the capital was moved effectively from Paris to Vichy, France. He maintained civil authority in the southwest part of France that was not occupied by German or Italian troops. The French navy and the French colonial empire, which included Algeria under French control, but for all intents and purposes, the government was just a puppet of the German Reich. Germany kept two million French soldiers in forced labor to ensure compliance. Petain was also anti-Semitic and sent many Jews to concentration camps in Germany. Not all

4 Ibid. pp.80, 112-116.

Frenchman were happy with the arrangement. A segment of the population became the French resistance under Charles de Gaulle which aligned with the allies.

Now all that stood in the way of complete victory was the British led by the newly elected Prime Minister, Winston Churchill. Hitler tried to beat down the British with air attacks, but the Royal Air Force kept that from happening. The British were also seafarers and the British navy prevented Germany from gaining superiority at sea. They bore the brunt of the war for a year until the Soviet Union, finally realizing their own vulnerability to German aggression, joined the Allied powers. That opened a front on the east. London was continuously bombed during that time. The British citizens hunkered down in shelters during the raids and then came out afterward and continued business as usual. One thing that happened during May that year helped boost British moral and dealt a serious blow to the German faith that they were invincible, the British naval ships came upon the impressive German Battleship, the Bismarck[5]. The ship was impressive by any standards. It was over 823 feet

5 Ibid, pp. 136-144.

long, 118 feet wide with a draft of over 32 feet and could travel at 30 knots. The Bismarck carried a complement of over 2000 officers and enlisted men. Her big 8 fifteen-inch guns could hit targets over twenty miles away making it exceedingly difficult to get close enough to her to inflict damage. The hull was so strong that small shells and torpedoes did little damage[6].6 After stalking the ship for a while, the British managed to disable her and finally sink her, losing the Hood and damage to other ships in the process. Also, during the summer of 1940, the British naval forces fought the Italian navy in the Mediterranean and won mastery in that region[7].

Bismarck

As in World War I, The United States remained neutral. As horrific as World War II was, it also saved our country. Our products were needed for the war effort. England and our own government spent huge amounts of money to support the war machine. That meant factories had to produce. That meant jobs. We intended to stay out of it but then on December 7, 1941, the Japanese attacked the US fleet at Pearl Harbor. The Japanese and Hitler underestimated

6 Bismarck-class battleship Wikipedia
7 Ibid, pp.145-147.

the ire of the American people. The next day, the United States declared war on Japan, Germany, and Italy and joined the Allies. The stage was set for the Allies to finally push the war back on Germany.

DAVID AND DENNIS MCINTYRE

CHAPTER 3:
DUTY

L averne joined the army April 4th, 1942. He felt that he needed to do his part for the war effort. He enlisted and received 4 months of basic training and then was sent as a member of a heavy machine gun squad off to war. He was assigned to Company M of the 26th Infantry. Laverne would see plenty of action all over the European theater.

His first campaign was in North Africa. The Russians who had joined the war the previous year in June of 1941 were now being severely beaten back by the German Blitzkrieg. Stalin was clamoring for another front to the west to relieve the pressure on his troops. America's president, Franklyn Roosevelt, pushed to have Dwight D. Eisenhower made supreme commander of the allied forces. Eisenhower wanted to start invasion in France, but Britain's Churchill wanted the attack to start in North Africa. The British General Montgomery had already been fighting the German General Rommel for more than a year and a half across Africa, without decisively beating the "Desert Fox". Churchill won out and plans were drawn up for the initial invasions to start in North Africa. That decision turned out to be particularly important because the American soldiers were nowhere ready to face the seasoned German army. They faced, instead, the Vichy French in North Africa who were not totally enamored with the Third Reich.

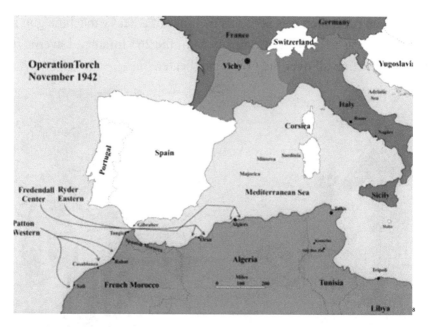

Campaigns in war are given names to keep track of everything and for historical purposes. The North African campaign was called for Operation

---

8 Ibid Rick Atkinson, pp. 24-25

"Torch"[9]. The planning and preparation for the event was a monumental undertaking. Approximately 125,000 American and British troops were involved in the landings[10]. Many of the American troops had to be put on ships and transported across the Atlantic Ocean along with all their gear, supplies, tanks, trucks, jeeps, ammunition, food, fuel, etc. They could not rely on anything being of use once they landed in North Africa. The following is a quote from Rick Atkinson, the Pulitzer Prize winning author of the Liberation Trilogy:

> *Into the holds went tanks and cannons, rubber boats and outboard motors, ammunition and machine guns, magnifying glasses and stepladders, alarm clocks and bicycles. Into the holds went: tractors, cement, asphalt, and more than a million gallons of gasoline, mostly in five-gallon tins. Into the holds went; thousands of miles of wire, well-digging machinery, railroad cars, 740,000 bottles of insect repellent, and 7,000 tons of coal in burlap bags. Into the holds went; black basketball shoes, 3,000 vehicles, loudspeakers, 16,000 feet of cotton rope, and $100,000 in gold coins, entrusted to George Patton personally. And into the holds went; a platoon of carrier pigeons, six flyswatters and sixty rolls of fly paper for each 1,000 soldiers, plus five pounds of rat poison per company[11].*

Besides the people and logistics problems, Eisenhower had to deal with personal animosities among the generals under his command. The British General Montgomery thought he should be in charge because he had been fighting the Germans for over a year and half and felt he was better qualified than this new American upstart by the name of Eisenhower. General George Patton did not like Montgomery. Some of the others had their own agendas. There was also the matter that the Vichy French in control of most of the landing sites did not like the British and many felt it would go better if the campaign was an American and not a British one. Eisenhower also had to bow to the wishes of two world leaders Churchill and President Roosevelt and the

---

9 Rick Atkinson "An Army at Dawn", Picador, Henry Holt and Company, New York, 2002, pp. 24-25.
10 Wikipedia.
11 Ibid. Rick Atkinson, P.33.

American Joint Chiefs of Staff. He had to be a soldier politician overseeing "Operation Torch" and for the rest of the war.

The timing, tides, weather, and a host of other things also had to be considered. In the end, it was decided that the forces would make a 3-pronged attack on the beaches of North Africa and secure the objectives between November 8-16, 1942. Patton would take his troops into Casablanca, A second attack would be made at 500 miles to the East led, in part, by General Teddy Roosevelt, the son of the former president of the same name, at Oran. A third landing would be made at Algiers another 260 miles further east. The final objective, however, was not any of those sites. It was Tunis in Tunisia another 500 miles even further east from Algiers. The 3- pronged attack was meant to prevent any chance that Rommel's army could get in behind the Americans heading for Tunis or be resupplied through ports on the Mediterranean to the west. The plan was to finally trap him in Tunisia. When you consider the distances, though, that would be like one force landing in Miami, another into Jacksonville, and another at Myrtle Beach with the final objective being an assault on New York City. They had to land and take everything with them. There were no gas stations along the way, no restaurants for food, no shopping areas, and you could not buy ammunition. Critical things like gasoline and ammunition had to be supplied from the rear or the army stopped.

Laverne, of course was oblivious to all the planning and drama. He just obeyed orders. He boarded the ship as ordered, made sure he had his personal stuff, and got ready to land on a beach. His unit, the 26th Infantry landed at Oran.

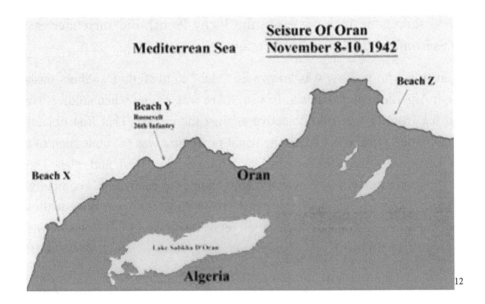

The Americans were cocky and had counted on the Vichy French surrendering easily. Instead, some of the French chose to fight. The greatest resistance was in the harbor at Oran. The 26th Infantry landed at a beach, designated beach Y, west of the port. The resistance at that point was much less allowing the troops to land with relatively few casualties. Meanwhile, Patton and his army were landing at Casablanca in Morocco and a third landing was in progress at Algiers where the resistance was the heaviest. The landing at Oran was especially important to Eisenhower. He wanted two airfields south of Oran captured quickly. Laverne and his fellow soldiers on the ground knew little more than what was happening right in front of them. On the first day, Oran was nearly surrounded with thousands of soldiers ashore with relatively light casualties. That wasn't true for all the battles. The ships entering the Oran harbor, for example, got hit hard even sunk. There were also errors. The navy transporting the troops and the landing craft operators had to rely on landmarks or poorly laid beacons to reach their assigned positions. Airborne paratroopers used what today would be very primitive methods of dead reckoning to reach their targets. There were no GPS systems in either case to determine exact positioning. Even with all the problems, the landings in North Africa were

---

12 Ibid Rick Atkinson, P.68.

deemed successful. In some cases, the Vichy French did surrender easily even welcoming the American liberators.

Laverne who by now was known as "Mac" to his fellow soldiers pushed through Algeria toward Tunisia. In war, there was a time when soldiers were put at the front to reach an objective against the enemy. That first objective was met when Oran was taken. The usual procedure was to rotate men to the rear where they could take showers, clean up, get a hot meal, and relax. Those were the good times where they could enjoy games or each other's company or even see the "sights". Tunisia was a priority so down time was done while on the move toward the objective. The men relaxed and wondered if the Germans would really be all that hard to beat.

CHAPTER 4:
TRIAL

The 26th had earned the companies first battle ribbon of the war referred to as the Algeria French Morocco campaign. The unit would earn 7 more before the war's end. The next one would not be so easy, Tunisia. The Americans up to this point had not really endured that much. They had seen some fighting, and a few had been wounded and even some had been killed, but they were not battle-hardened soldiers yet. They were too cocky, too well treated and fed, and had not yet made the transition to killers. Every soldier bearing a weapon in war must change his mindset from killing is wrong to killing is necessary to fulfill the greater objectives, in this case liberation. They will need that instinct to defeat the already hardened German forces. That mindset, though, has consequences. Everything a person accepts as Ok and right also means it is Ok and right for others to do it back to them. A liar expects everyone else will be lying. A thief worries that some else will steal from him. A killer will sleep with his gun nearby afraid that someone else will do him in. In war, the soldier must sleep with his gun nearby. When the soldier returns from war, the transition back to a civilian mindset is difficult and may lead to PTSD. Mac's company as well as all the other Americans were about to be hardened.

After landing and securing Oran and the other objectives, the army made their way toward Tunisia. That campaign would take about 6 months from November 12, 1942 to May 13, 1943. It took time to move the army that distance and deal with all the resistance along the way. It also took time to rebuild ports and airfields that were damaged or destroyed. It took time to unload supplies for the war effort and move them to where they are needed. It also took time to correct all the mistakes and there apparently were quite a few.

By February 1943, the army was moving into western Tunisia. Rommel and the German army were on the eastern side. General Fredendall directed the placement of defenses around Faid and Kasserine passes. Those defenses proved to be totally inadequate against Rommel's forces. The Germans had fortified Faid pass and one battalion of the Colonel Stark's 26th Infantry ran into deadly fire.

> *"The battalion scaled one ridge, then a second, only to be pinned down for the rest of the day by an impenetrable wall of Axis fire from the third crest."*[13]

An American armored staged a frontal assault on Faid pass and were promptly strafed by German Messerschmitt planes as they entered the pass. It was a trap with the German 88 guns firing on them from 3 sides. Within 10 minutes half the American tanks were on fire. The rest retreated as fast as they could. The infantry tried again and were beaten back. Faid pass was gone. Everybody was blaming everybody else for the failed attacks. Intelligence had warned the armored division's commanding Brigadier General McQuillan of the placement of the big 88 guns. Both the infantry and the armored unit blamed each other for lack of support[14].

---

13 Ibid. Rick Atkinson, p.310.
14 Ibid Rick Atkinson, pp. 316-317.

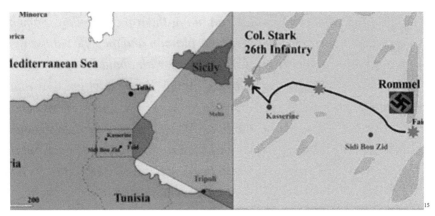

Mac was in the middle of or near the action somewhere. It was his 26th Infantry under Colonel Stark that bore the brunt of the failed infantry attack. Then it got worse. The Americans had to retreat to Sidi Bou Zid. The Germans counterattacked. Within minutes the American tanks were annihilated. Units began to fall one after another.

> *"Soldiers scooped foxholes with their helmets or clawed at the ground until their fingers bled. 'All around me comrades were being machined gunned from tanks,' one soldier recalled. 'Their screams were faintly heard due to the terrific explosions.'"16*

> *"It looks like," suggested one tanker, "like a dryland Dunkirk."17*

After it was all over, Mac sent a letter back to his sweetheart Rae describing a first-hand account of the event. Rae likely had to sit down and recover a bit from the shock of his nonchalant presentation of the facts. The following is an excerpt.

> *"They say that we can tell of some of our experiences now......I suppose you would like to hear of my being captured first. It happened in the last few days of fighting here. We were attacking a long range of mountains. We were attached to a rifle company. The rifle company made it to the top of one hill just at daybreak. We had been coming up*

15 Ibid Rick Atkinson, p. 358.
16 Ibid Rick Atkinson, p.341.
17 Ibid. Rick Atkinson, p. 342

through a wheat field which ran along the top of a gulley. Somehow, we lost connection with part of our platoon and the rifle company. The fire got too hot where we were so along with about 15 of our platoon, I crawled down to the side of the gulley. It was daylight now and we found that we could go no further forward. The gulley curved enough so that we were safe on the bank but not up any further. Found out later that the platoon leader had tried to send a runner back but there was a crossfire from up in the gulley and a hill on our left, so we had to turn back. They fired some artillery and air burst at us during the day.

Part of the rifle company were in a bad position up front, so they made a run for the creek about 300 yards in back of us where they dug in. They were fired on as they went back but no one got hit. We could have gone with them but thought we had better stay near our platoon leader in case he wanted us.

Morgan and I decided to dig a foxhole together as the ground was very hard and by doing so, we hoped to get done quicker. It took us most of the day and if their artillery hadn't kept encouraging us, we would have given it up. It came in very handy later and probably saved us from getting killed or hurt.

Late in the afternoon we crawled in our hole to wait for darkness. Having had no sleep the night before and only 3 hours the night before that, it isn't strange that we fell asleep. We awoke to find ourselves completely surrounded. The rest of the platoon had taken off some of them going up into the wheat field again and some straight up the gulley. The Jerries had set a mortar up in the gulley right below us. They were firing flares at different spots and spaying all over with lead. Two hand grenades went off near us. One of our men had been hit in the leg and was crying for help about 20 feet away. We were trying to make up our minds what to do. We lay flat in the hole for a few minutes in hopes that they would move forward but no such luck. Morgan is a first-aid man and carries no gun. Two of the Jerries' started straight for our hole in answer to a call from a party on the opposite side. Maybe I did wrong by not trying to get one or two of them but when you are with a man who doesn't have a gun, you can't very well endanger his life too. We let them get within a foot or two of the hole before giving up. It was quite dark except for tracers and flares. They searched us briefly for weapons and we asked to fix up the wounded man nearby. They spoke a little English. I still think most of them had lain all day in nearby bushes. We had taken two prisoners earlier whom we had spotted on the other side of the gulley about 100 yards away. One of them had taken a few pot shots at us and we couldn't at first figure out where they came from. I hope I'm never caught like that again without at least one grenade. It might have been a different story if I could have tossed a grenade in among that mortar crew.

We had to put the wounded man on a blanket and follow our captors. Had gone about 100 yards and were wondering how we were going to make it when our captors stopped and hollered. An answering hello came, and two more Jerries brought 5 more prisoners down. They were the ones who had tried to get away up the gulley. One man had a piece of shrapnel in his foot which he had gotten early in the day but hadn't been able to get back to the medics for treatment.

So now, with two helping him and four carrying the blanket we started off again. We walked for over 10 miles dragging and carrying the poor wounded fellow over rocks, bushes and when one of us would trip, we'd bounce him on the ground. I don't blame them for wanting to hurry as our artillery was coming close at times. We were all tuckered out and I thought my arms would never be able to hold the blanket another step. The only relief we could get was changing around and helping the other wounded man. It sprinkled a little and one fellow tried to quench his thirst by sucking his shirt and cap. I tried to catch a little in my helmet, but it wouldn't rain hard enough for that. Our captors had no water. They did stop long enough to borrow a drink from another party for the wounded. I got so tired I found myself trying to walk over small trees. The blanket finally gave out from being dragged so much.

By this time, we had gotten back to where they had some wounded who were being carried back by donkeys. We had tried to get them to let us put him on one, but it wasn't until the blanket gave out that they would. It wasn't very much fun holding him on, but it was better for him and easier for us.

We finally got back to their headquarters. There they gave us some grayish black bread, cold coffee, and water. They had taken our cigarettes but gave us some Jerry cigarettes there. After a short wait, a truck drove up and we made the wounded as comfortable as we could in the front while we got near the back with our captors. At their field hospital they gave immediate attention to the wounded. Our guides then took us to a main highway where they hailed ride on a huge halftrack. They carry 15 or 20 people and have a track on the rear like a tank.

There were now six of us and our captors left us in the charge of the driver and his companion. About 10 miles out we noticed artillery shells landing near the road. The two Jerrys put on their helmets and then the driver stepped on the gas. One shell hit near throwing dirt in our faces and blowing out the front tire. Thought we were headed for the ditch, but he got control of it and drove on to a safe place to change the tire. It was then we got split up. Morgan and two others being put in a tank and the rest of us in a truck. The road was lined with all kinds of vehicles all in a hurry. There were dead mules and overturned carts along the way. We got to Tunis safely and were put in a schoolhouse on the outskirts. Were released a few hours later by the British there being very little fighting for the city itself. It seemed funny to be guarding the fellows who a moment before had been guarding us. An American officer who had been prisoner took charge of things.

After that temporary setback, Mac and his buddies were treated to a good time in Tunis. Meanwhile, the American forces were pushed all the way back to Kasserine pass and Colonel Stark was told to hold the line there. The enemy began to infiltrate past the U.S. lines.

> *"Enemy artillery fell with greater insistence as the night deepened. 'the worst of it all was to see some of your best buddies next to you being shot down or blown up,' observed an engineer corporal. 'I never knew that there could possibly be so many shells in the air at the same time and so many explosions near you and still come out alive.' Compounding the terror was a new German weapon deployed for the first time, the Nebelwerfer, a six-barrel mortar that "stonked" targets with a half-dozen 75 pound high-explosive rounds soon known as screaming meemies or moaning minnies because the wail they made in flight was said to resemble 'a lot of women sobbing their hearts out.'"[18]*

> *"The American collapse began.... Companies disintegrated into platoons, platoons into squads, squads into solitary foot soldiers chased to the rear by screaming meemies."[19]*

> *"All day long, hundreds of fleeing soldiers from Stark's wrecked command drifted through Thala yelling, 'He's right behind us!' No one needed to ask who 'he' was."[20]*

The British armored division came to the rescue at Thala. They held the line against Rommel's advancing panzer division. The Americans then rallied and finally stopped Rommel and put him in retreat. The American losses exceeded 6,000 of 30,000 men engaged in battle. Fredendall's corps lost 183 tanks, 104 half-tracks, more than 200 guns, and 500 jeeps and trucks. German losses were light, only 201 dead[21]. Kasserine is now considered one the greatest American defeats of all time not just in World War II. The British were not so sure they had a strong ally in the Americans. Montgomery was even more

18 Ibid. Rick Atkinson p. 371.
19 Ibid. Rick Atkinson, p.372.
20 Ibid, Rick Atkinson, p. 383.
21 Ibid. Rick Atkinson, p. 389.

convinced that he, not Eisenhower, should be in charge. The Americans hung their heads. Eisenhower removed Fredendall from command and placed his command under Patton. It was gloomy for a couple of months but now the battle-hardened Americans were determined to fight back. They held their ground, the artillery got better at knocking out tanks and reigning fire down on the Germans. The Americans began winning the battles in Tunisia town by town, hill by hill. Mac's unit, the 26th Infantry, helped the line advance east of El Guettar, Tunisia.

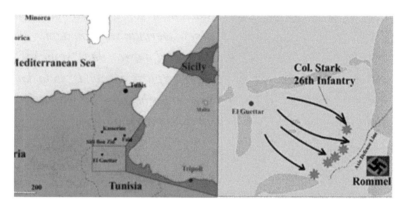

The British and American forces began pushing German army northward until by May 13, 1943 the Germans experienced their own version of Dunkirk. Roughly 250,000 Germans were captured. Rommel by that time had been ordered out of the fight. The Americans were redeemed and had their revenge for Kasserine.

> "At a price of 70,000 casualties 'one continent had been redeemed,' in Churchill's phrase. But more than territory could be claimed. The gains were most profound for the Americans, in their first campaign against the Wehrmacht. Four U.S. divisions now had combat experience in five variants of Euro-Mediterranean warfare: expeditionary, amphibious, mountain, desert, and urban. Troops had learned the importance of terrain, of combined arms, of aggressive patrolling, of stealth, of massed armor. They now knew what it was like to be bombed, shelled, and machine- gunned, and to fight on. They provided Eisenhower with

a blooded hundred thousand, 'high-grade stock from which we must breed with the utmost rapidity,' as one general urged."[22]

Mac and his 26th Infantry now had another battle ribbon to their credit. They had become killers.

"The blood was up in these mercurial people. They were further inflamed by wide-eyed atrocity tales of German bayoneting prisoners. At El Guetiar 'we really learned to hate,' a sergeant in the 26th Infantry later wrote. 'The hatred for the Krauts carried through to the rest of the Tunisian campaign, Sicily, France, Belgium, through Germany, into the Harz mountains, and Czechoslovakia.' An officer in the 6th Infantry concluded, 'A soldier is not effective until he has learned to hate. When he lives for one thing, to kill the enemy, he becomes of value."[23]

After the Tunisian campaign, the 1st Division, which included the 26th Infantry, returned to Algeria where they let off a lot of built-up steam. There was a "trail of looted wine shops and outraged mayors" and some soldiers even fired at Arab peasants.[24]

When Mac was finally discharged in 1945, there was a curious note in his record that there were 9 days lost under AW 107. That designation was common among the soldiers in World War II and usually meant that the soldier had gone on a wild drinking spree without authorization. It was war and the soldiers were forgiven, but they had to make up the time lost. Maybe Mac joined his buddies for a little R and R in Algeria.

There was another interesting side note in the North African and Tunisian campaigns. The large contingent of American soldiers brought huge amounts of American dollars to Africa. The United States feared that, if the Germans prevailed, they could have access to large amounts of U.S currency. To remedy the situation, the U.S printed African versions of the currency. It looked the

---

22 Ibid Rick Atkinson, p. 537.
23 Ibid Rick Atkinson, p. 462.
24 Rick Atkinson, "The Day of Battle", Picador Henry Holt and Company, 2007, p. 95

same except that there was a yellow circle instead of the normal green one on the right. The idea was that if the Germans gained the upper hand, The U.S. could devalue that special currency and thwart the German plans.

Soldiers in the war also collected examples of foreign currency. It was common practice for them to sign individual bills and tape the bills together. It was a way for them to never forget who they served with on the battlefield. Mac had one such bill, an Algerian note signed that way.

CHAPTER 5:

HEROES

The next big campaign was Sicily known as Operation "Husky". This landing, scheduled for July 9, 1943, was to be the largest ever attempted. It would involve 3,000 Allied ships and boats, three times as many soldiers to put ashore as in Operation Torch.[25] In preparation for the campaign, soldiers were packed onto ships where they were filthy, lived in dirty clothes, had to put up with filthy toilets, army inspectors found vermin in the food, and there was a shortage of vomit buckets. The lack of buckets was especially hard on those like Mac that were prone to seasickness. Soldiers began to be nostalgic for the tangerines and pomegranates of North Africa. Soldiers were given "A Soldiers Guide to Sicily" which described:

> *"the heat filth, and disease in such detail that the 26th Infantry's regimental log concluded the island must be a 'hellhole inhabited by folks who were too poor to leave or too ignorant to know there were better places.'*[26]

Before the landings in Morocco, there had been a ferocious Atlantic storm which subsided before the amphibious assault began. This time the weather threatened again. High northwesterly winds and steep seas were predicted the day before the landing, which reached a gale-force thirty-knot wind speed. The

25 Rick Atkinson, p. 33.
26 Ibid. Rick Atkinson, p.62.

seas would be high. The landing craft referred to as LST's (Landing Ship Tank or the sailor's version Large Slow Target), were square-bowed flat bottom craft that did not do well in heavy seas. They had to be flat bottom so they could get in close to land as possible on the beaches carrying their heavy loads of men and equipment. Some described them as floating "shoeboxes". They would lurch up from the sea with one wave, drop with a thud, a heavy shutter on the next, and could roll over 45 degrees side to side. They were extremely dangerous to the soldiers who tried to board them from a mother ship. Soldiers riding them to the beach would be drenched in seawater and vomit from all those who were prone to seasickness. Mac certainly contributed his share of vomit. Once on route to the shore, it was extremely hard to keep them headed in the right direction. Every wave could potentially knock them off course. They were powered by two engines and if they lost one, the operator would have to turn 180 degrees around and hope he could get back on course. A paperback book titled "What to Do Aboard a Transport" stated:

> *"the sickest landlubber laughs at some other fellow with a green look about the gills."*
>
> *No one was laughing. 'All of us are miserable, anxious, jam-packed, overloaded and wet,' a soldier in the 26th infantry wrote. 'No place to be sick except on one another. There are no heroes, just misery."*[27]

A good many men were lost just trying to launch the LST's. Nearly every mother ship lost at least one landing craft.[28] To the average soldier like Mac, it seemed like nothing was ever going right. Their skepticism spawned an acronym describing their lowered expectations: SNAFU, situation normal all fouled up. Of course, their version had slightly different wording. There were other versions of it as well like FUBAR, fouled up beyond all recognition.[29]

The gale force winds the day before the landing did help because the Italian defenders never expected an amphibious assault under such conditions, but it was very foreboding for the Allies. The weather did die down the next day,

---

27 Ibid. Rick Atkinson, p. 65.
28 Ibid, Rick Atkinson, p. 71.
29 Ibid. Rick Atkinson, p. 36.

but the sea was still up making it more difficult for the LST's to land. There was another problem for the soldiers; each man was to carry a pack on his back with all the necessary ammunition, grenades, tools, and supplies that he would need. That pack weighed 82 pounds.[30] If the LST did not go in far enough onto the beach, the men may have to jump into water that was over their heads. If they did, they would promptly sink to the bottom. Then they would have to jettison their packs or drown.

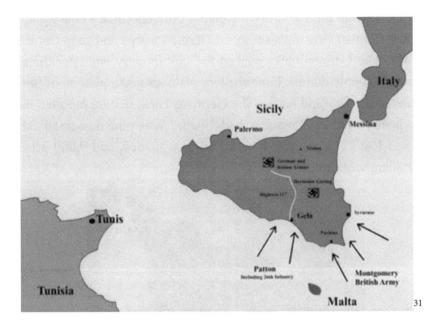

The Americans under General George Patton were assigned to land around Gela while The British army under General Montgomery were to land on the southeastern corner of Sicily. The 26th was part of the 1st division commanded by Major General Terry Allen and assistant commander Brigadier General Ted Roosevelt. The 26th Infantry was assigned to land at Gela in the first wave. When the assault began, the Italians blew up a long segment of the thousand-foot Gela pier eliminating any chance for an easy landing. Italian gunners then trained their guns on the 26th as they closed within 100 yards of the shore.[32]

30 Ibid. Rick Atkinson, p. 78.
31 Ibid Rick Atkinson. p.73
32 32 Ibid. Rick Atkinson, p. 79.

Mac and his fellow soldiers realized that the landing was not going to be as easy as Oran. Still by the second day, 50,000 U.S. troops and 5,000 vehicles had landed, casualties had been modest, there were stacks of enemy dead many of them German, and a sizable number of mostly Italian prisoners.[33] Ted landed on the beach at Gela with the first wave and was well respected by the troops under him.

After securing the beach, the 26th was assigned to move up highway 117 north of Gela while the 16th army traveled a different route to the right. They would face Herman Goering's seasoned German troops and soon came under tank attack. The German tanks pushed the 26th Infantry and later threatened the Infantry's supply dumps. Four artillery platoons and a platoon of Sherman tanks entered the fray and pushed the Germans back. Goring reported back to his headquarters that counterattack had failed.[34] When the dust finally settled, Goring had lost 43 tanks, 630 men killed or wounded, and 9,000 prisoners, mostly Italian, were taken.[35]

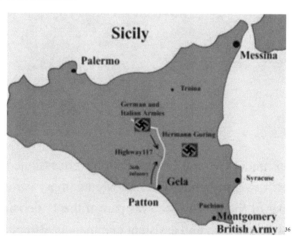

The troops learn to expect SNAFU's and there were some. Twenty-three hundred men were supposed to parachute in to help the Big Red One as the

---

33 Ibid. Rick Atkinson. pp. 86-87.
34 Ibid. Rick Atkinson, pp.102-103.
35 Ibid. Rick Atkinson. p.104.
36 Ibid. Rick Atkinson, p. 97

1st Division was called. The C-47's carrying them had to fly over the landing fleet to their drop zones. Thinking they were enemy aircraft, some of the fleet opened fire on them destroying 23 planes and causing 410 casualties. It was one of the worst friendly fire episodes in modern warfare.[37] It would not be the last.

War corrupts men and some take things too far. It is one thing to kill the enemy while he is trying to kill you. It is quite another to murder prisoners of war after they surrendered. A sergeant in one company separated out 9 prisoners from group of captured men and then borrowed a Thompson submachine gun and killed the rest, 37 men in all. In another incident a Captain ordered 36 Italian prisoners shot by firing squad. The sergeant was later tried for his crimes and given life imprisonment, which was later commuted with a loss of rank and the captain was court marshaled.[38]

The summer heat and malaria along with insufficient beds (only 3,300 for 200,000 soldiers now in Sicily) also added problems. In one of those beds was a soldier from Mac's 26th unit by the name of Charles H. Kuhl. He was diagnosed as having a "Psychoneurosis anxiety state-moderate severe. Later, it was determined he had malaria, and chronic diarrhea. Patton visited him and asked him where he was hurt. The soldier shrugged and *said:*

> *"I guess I can't take it." Patton slapped the man across the face with his folded gloves. "You coward, you get out of this tent!" he shouted. "You can't stay in here with these brave, wounded Americans." Grabbing Kuhl by the collar, he dragged him to the tent entrance and shoved him out with a finishing kick from his cavalry boot.*

Patton slapped another man, Private Paul G. Bennett suffering from a similar disorder later. [39]

The army could not keep the slapping incidents secret. The press had a field day against Patton and Eisenhower was forced to discipline him. Patton later

---

37 Ibid. Rick Atkinson, pp.105-109.
38 Ibid. Rick Atkinson, pp116-121.
39 Ibid. Rick Atkinson, pp. 144=147.

lost his command for a while after the Sicilian campaign. He later went back to both men and apologized.

The goal was to push the Germans completely out of Sicily and so both the British and the Americans set their sights on Messina, in the northeast corner of Sicily. Patton moved his army up the western part of Sicily while Montgomery moved up the eastern part. It was a race and Patton wanted to win it; he did not like Montgomery. They pushed hard. The closer they got to Messina, the greater the resistance. Mac's unit was ordered to loop north around Troina while the 18th Infantry came up from the south.

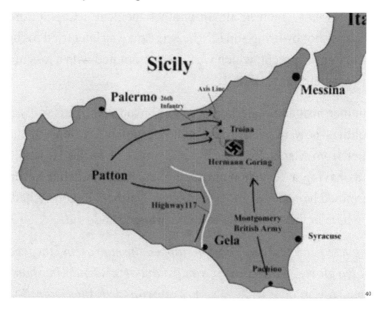

Hills were won and lost, won again, and lost again. By now the Germans had dug in so deep that even observers droning overhead could not spot the smokeless powder from their artillery and antitank guns. To break the stalemate, Allen ordered a renewed assault in the early minutes of August 3, with the attack weighted in the south. At daybreak, the 16th Infantry was pinned down by gashing German fire ... Progress was no better in the north. Troops from the 26th Infantry fought with grenades, pistols, rifle butts up and down a bitter knoll

40 Ibid. Rick Atkinson, p.156.

known as Hill 1035. The sharp pops of detonating mines were often followed by the howl that signified another severed foot or leg. Not until full dark, at eleven p.m., could the wounded be evacuated. Brush fires made the scorching days hotter still, and putrid German bodies polluted a creek trickling through a ravine.[41]

Rifle companies throughout the first division had been reduced by two-thirds fighting. One company commander lay with a radio a mile north of Troina, as his unit was overrun and called in artillery barrages to within 50 yards of his foxhole. The 1st Division planned a final assault for the next day to finally remove the Germans. When they finally went out, they found the Germans had withdrawn. Goering's Panzer Division had lost more than 1600 men.[42] Troina was devastated.

"They found 'a town of horror, alive with weeping, hysterical men, women and children,' wrote Herbert Matthews of The New York Times; he described a scene that would recur all the way to Bologna: on 'torn streets, heaps of rubble that had been houses, grief, horror and pain.' Dead soldiers, German and American, were 'covered with a carpet of maggots that made it look as though the corpses were alive and twitching,' a 16th Infantry officer reported. 'You couldn't get the smell of the dead out of your hair, and all you could do with your clothes was burn them.' A 26th Infantry captain, Donald V. Helgeson, stared at a charred German motor crew. 'This ain't very good for the troops 'morale,' Helgeson said. His first sergeant disagreed, 'It's great for morale. They're Germans, aren't they?' A GI sliced the Wehrmacht belt buckle from a dead grenadier and declared that 'Gott mit Uns changed sides."[43]

It was common practice for soldiers to take such souvenirs. Mac acquired his share of them and brought them back home with him. He never said anything about where or how he got them.

---

41 Ibid. Rick Atkinson, pp. 156-157.
42 Ibid . Rick Atkinson, pp. 157-158
43 Ibid.Rick Atkinson. p. 158.

Mac's Souvenirs

In August 5[th]1943, Mac's unit was awarded a Presidential Unit Citation GO #36.[44] That citation was reserved for those units that displayed extraordinary heroism. It was the equivalent of a Distinguished Service Cross for an individual.

> *"The unit must display gallantry, determination, and spirit de corps in accomplishing a mission under extremely difficult and hazardous conditions so as to set it apart from and above other units in the same campaign."[45]*

---

44 Written on Laverne's Honorable Discharge Papers 12 September 1945.
45 Wikipedia Presential Unit Citation (United States) as quoted from declassified government documents.

Presidential Unit Citation medal

There were two more casualties of Troina, Terry Allen and Ted Roosevelt were relieved of command. It was a blow especially to Roosevelt to leave the 26th Infantry because he had commanded that unit in World War I.[46]

Patton and Montgomery pushed on to Messina. They were ultimately successful, but in war there is always a cost.

> *"The butcher's bill was dear for both sides. American battle casualties totaled 8,800, including 2,237 killed in action, plus another 13,000 hospitalized for illness. The British battle tally of 12,800 included 2,721 killed. Axis dead and wounded approached 29,000-an Italian count 4,300 German and 4,700 Italian graves in Sicily. But it was the 140,000 Axis soldiers captured, nearly all of them Italian, who severely tilted the final casualty totals."[47]*

---

46 Ibid. Rick Atkinson. pp. 159-160.
47 Ibid. Rick Atkinson. PP. 172-173.

CHAPTER 6:
COURAGE

T he 26th Infantry was taken out of the front lines for a well-deserved time of rest and recuperation. Meanwhile other army divisions would carry the war up the boot of Italy. The assault on Italy was a long-drawn-out battle lasting from September 1943 to almost May of 1945. Anzio may be the most famous of the battle locations. The Italian campaign may also have been the costliest for both sides with 320,000 Allied and 330,000 German casualties.[48] Mac and his buddies, thankfully, missed that campaign. They would be needed, but not until the landings on Normandy, designated Operation Overlord. There was a great deal of preparation to be done first.

An elaborate deception was also orchestrated to fool the Germans as to where, when, and from which ports the assault would originate. General Patton, who had gotten a "slap" on the wrist for his publicized slapping of soldiers was relieved of combat command and given the task of leading the ruse. The Germans knew Patton and expected that he would be leading a good part of any assault on the northern beaches. Eisenhower and the joint chiefs thought they could use that to fool the Germans. Fifteen hundred Allied deceivers used phony radio traffic to suggest a fictional army was forming with divisions in Scotland. The deception suggested an attack on Norway with a larger invasion to attack France in mid-July 150 miles north east of the actual planned Overlord

48 Wikipedia The Italian Campaign (World War II)

beaches. They fashion decoy landing craft from oil drums and canvas. The British leaked false information to known German spies. They set up fake tanks and other equipment in the false staging area to further convince German aerial observers. The radio operators kept a continuous broadcast of fake radio chatter. A Lieutenant Clifton James of the Royal Army Pay Corps, who looked a lot like the British General Montgomery, was dressed like Montgomery complete with a black beret. He was sent to Gibraltar and then to Algiers just before the actual chosen date for the Normandy landing. The Germans knew that any big assault would have to include Montgomery. The hope was that "Montgomery" seen in public in Gibraltar and Algiers, would convince them that the invasion was not imminent.[49]

Meanwhile, soldiers added seasick pills, vomit bags, lifebelts, etc. to their packs which made the average combat load to almost 70 pounds.

> *"A company commander in Dorset with the 116th Infantry, bound for Omaha Beach, reported that his men were 'loping and braying about the camp under their packs, saying that as long as they were loaded like jackasses they might as well sound like them.'"*[50]

The largest amphibious fleet ever would be assembled for Normandy with nearly 7,000 ships, including landing craft and barges, in the armada.[51] The preparations had to be done in secret so as not alert the Germans where and when the battle was to commence. It would be an extremely difficult operation anyway as the British were aware from their experiences at Dunkirk. A whole host of things had to be considered. It had to be in a warmer month of the year. Soldiers would not be able to deal with the freezing waters in winter. June was chosen. Amphibious fleets needed winds less than 18 mph, or it would be a disaster for the landing craft. Pilots wanted a cloud 2500 foot ceiling and visibility no less than 3 miles, so they could see where to drop the paratroopers or their bombing loads. GPS had not been established yet, so pilots had to

---

49 Rick Atkinson, "The Guns at Last Light", Picador Henry Holt and Company, 2014, pp. 26-27
50 Ibid. Rick Atkinson, p.27.
51 Ibid. Rick Atkinson, p.29.

navigate by visible landmarks. Paratroopers needed winds of less than 20 mph, to reduce than chance of death just from the jump itself. The tides had to be right. The tides at Normandy were the largest of any of the amphibious landings with the difference between low tide to high tide could be over twenty feet. That meant that an exposed beach at low tide could be 20 or more feet underwater just 6 hours later at high tide. The soldiers, when they landed, would have to move very quickly to higher ground. They did not want to be caught exposed out in the open. The initial D-day was set at June 5, 1944.

> *"Weather charts resembled conditions typical of midwinter rather than early summer; depression L5, now skulking toward Shetland Islands, would produce the lowest atmospheric pressure recorded in the British Isles during June in the twentieth century. In a few hours complete overcast would blanket southern England, with a ceiling as low as five hundred feet and westerly winds up to thirty miles per hour at Force 6. Conditions for D-Day on June 5 had deteriorated from 'most unpromising' to 'quite impossible.'"*[52]

Eisenhower postponed the landing 24 hours, hoping the winds would die down. The next day he had to make the decision to go or not to go. Any more delay, and he would have to wait 2 more weeks for the tide to be right and risk that the Germans would find out. It was tense, but the decision was a go for June 6. The ships left port and the low visibility helped hide the approaching assault from the Germans.

> *"... the churlish open Chanel tested the seaworthiness of every landing vessel. Flat-bottomed LST's showed 'a capacity for rolling all ways at once' and smaller LCI- Landing Craft Infantry-revealed why it was widely derided as a Lousy Civilian Idea. Worse yet was the LCT, capable of only six knots in a millpond and half that into a head sea.*
>
> *Even the Navy acknowledged that 'the LCT is not an ocean- going craft due to poor sea-keeping facilities, low speed, and structural*

---

52 Ibid. Rick Atkinson, p.32.

weakness'; the latter quality included being bolted together in three sections so that the vessel 'gave an ominous impression of being liable to buckle in the middle.'[53]

infantrymen-landing-craft-Omaha-Beach-D-Day-June-6-1944

The soldiers were once again severely bounced around in the heavy seas slipping and sliding again in the concoction of saltwater and vomit heading for Normandy beaches. They would land on 5 beaches in Northeastern France. Montgomery would take his British and Canadian forces in on the 3 easternmost beaches while General Bradley would direct the Americans onto the 2 westernmost beaches designated as Utah and Omaha.

---

53 Ibid. Rick Atkinson, p.37.

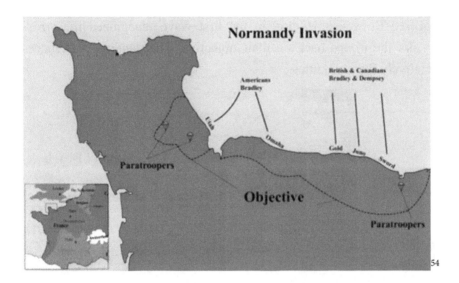

54

The invasion was preceded by 800 planes dropping 13,000 American paratroopers behind the lines to help eliminate German resistance to the troops landing by sea. The low cloud cover made it exceedingly difficult to navigate and see exactly where to make the jumps. Gliders were used to carry paratroopers piloted by inexperienced pilots who desperately searched the ground for their designated landing sites. Meanwhile, the Germans alerted to the attack opened with artillery fire. Many were killed before they left their planes. Most of the paratroops would miss their landing sites.

The British faired only a little better.[55]

> *"Yet this day would be famous even before it dawned, in no small measure because of the gutful men who had come to war by air. Beset by mischance, confounded by disorder, they mostly did what they were asked to do. Now the battle would hang on those who came by sea."*[56]

The forces that were supposed to land at Utah beach, ended up landing 2,000 yards off at the wrong beach. That proved to be a blessing, because that part of the French shoreline was not well defended by the Germans. Brigadier

54 Ibid. Rick Atkinson, p.44.
55 Ibid. Rick Atkinson, pp. 45-53
56 Ibid. Rick Atkinson, p. 53

General Ted Roosevelt landing in the first wave recognized the error and quickly got the troops back on their objective. That landing was successful with relatively few casualties.[57]

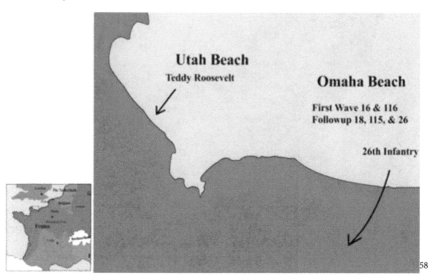

Omaha Beach, later referred to as "Bloody Omaha" and "Hell's Beach", was a totally different story. Engineers had to go in first, jump into 54-degree water and quickly clear out as many of the over three thousand booby-trapped obstacles to clear paths for the landing craft to follow. It had to be on a rising tide so that landing craft would not be stranded on a falling tide. They had to complete their task quickly because the tide was coming in at a rate of about one foot every eight minutes. The difference between low and high tide was over twenty feet. The shoreline was heavily defended.

Some landing craft were sunk before they reached the beach. By seven A.M. only about a third of the gaps had been opened through the obstacles now being inundated by the rising tide at a cost of over half of the engineers.[59]

---

57 Ibid. Rick Atkinson, p.61.
58 Ibid. Rick Atkinson, p.617
59 Ibid, Rick Atkinson, pp.64-68.

Omaha Beach Obstacles

German Machine Gun Overlooking Omaha Beach

"German machine guns-with a sound one GI compared to 'a venetian blind being lifted up rapidly'-perforated the beach killing the wounded and rekilling the dead. All thirty-two soldiers in one boat, LCA-1015, were slaughtered, including their captain. A lieutenant shot in the brain continued to direct his troops until, a survivor recounted, 'he sat down and held his head in the palm of his hand before falling over

dead.' Wounded men jabbed themselves with morphine or shrieked for medics, one of whom used safety pins to close a gaping leg wound.... Medics found that 'the greater portion of the dead had died of bullet wounds through the head'.... 'Fire was coming from everywhere, big and little stuff' a soldier in E company recalled. Moved to computation by the demented shooting, one sergeant calculated that the beach was swept with 'at least twenty thousand bullets and shells per minute.'"[60]

"By 8:30 A.M. the Omaha assault had stalled.... 'Face downwards, as far as eyes could see in either direction,' a 16th Infantry surgeon later wrote, 'were the huddled bodies of men living, wounded, and dead, as tightly packed together as layers of cigars in a box.'"[61]

Seeing the dilemma of the troops on the beach, a dozen destroyers came so close to the beach that some of their keels scraped bottom. From there they could fire at point blank range on the defenders on the cliffs.

According to Rick Atkinson, Mac and the 26th Infantry was ordered onto Omaha beach later. Other historical sources said that the 26th landed later at Utah beach.[62] This author tends to believe Rick Atkinson is correct especially because of the map showing troop movement inland off the beach. Either way, though, God was with Mac and his buddies keeping them from the murderous fire on Omaha beach. He could not be protected, however, from seeing the results. Bullet ridden; sometimes mutilated bodies of fellow soldiers were everywhere. Some even huddled together in a desperate effort to escape the killing fire. Mac and his fellow soldiers had to be thinking that it could have been them. It was a horrible sight one that may well have engendered sleepless nights and nightmares. Nobody talked about PTSD at that time. Soldiers just had to take it and move on.

The Allied forces were on French coast but for a while, did not penetrate far inland. Seven weeks after the D-Day landing on Normandy, thirty-three allied divisions had only penetrated 30 miles inland at a cost of 122,000 casualties

60 Ibid. Rick Atkinson, p.69
61 Ibid. Rick Atkinson, p. 70.
62 Ibid. Rick Atkinson, p.75.

(killed, wounded, or missing). The breakthrough came with Operation Cobra, which was to be "a sledgehammer blow on a narrow front"[63] south of the American beach landings. It was successful and opened the way to steady advances. There also was another landing on the shores of southern France during August.[64] Since the landing at Normandy on June 6th German losses exceeded 400,000, half of them prisoners.[65] Allied casualties topped 134,000, the British, Canadians and Poles totaled 91,000. There had been 600,000 tons of Allied bombs dropped on France causing between 50,000 and 67,000 French deaths. A side note, there had been a failed attempt on Hitler's life that made Hitler angry enough to try Rommel for treason. He was not a part of the attempt but knew about it. He swallowed cyanide to end his life. Hitler, as deceitful as always, sent a six-floral wreath to the funeral to mourn the loss of a great German hero.[66]

Mac had left a hand-written poem that appears in his own handwriting that kind of describes how he felt at the end of 1944 perhaps in anticipation of the victory in 1945. It is not known if he was the author, but he might have been. He was familiar with the big guns mentioned in the poem. It was entitled 1944.

1944

Now I have a home I call my own
Though some people wouldn't call it a home
It's not built for beauty I do admit
And its full of sand, dust and grit
The roof does leak that is true
And most of my company is a bug or two
It's not too hard to make my home you know
Just one little shell and down I go
For my home is a fox hole in the ground

---

63 Ibid. Rick Atkinson, pp. 137, 139
64 Ibid. Rick Atkinson, p. 188.
65 Ibid. Rick Atkinson, p. 181.
66 Ibid. Rick Atkinson. p. 182.

And in it I fell sort of safe and sound
When I emerge it cautiously?
For there may be a sniper in a nearby tree
It's not from him I'm in the ground
For in the air is a funny sound
A sound quite familiar to me
For I heard in Africa and Sicily
A sound that's made by an 88
If you meet up with one, it's the Pearly Gate
When I hear that sound in my home, I lay
Hoping and praying it's not wrecked today
There is a sound I like to hear
A message to Jerry that should be clear
Telling him to run for his life
To pray for himself not his kiddies or wife
Our artillery has him spotted and it is my guess
That before the day is ended Hitler's boys will be less
For I really don't see how they can stay alive
If they are anywhere near the burst of a 155
But let the shells soar overhead
For now, it is time to go to bed
To try and get a little sleep
Before a sentry's watch I keep
For we guard our home night and day
And fight for them and the USA
Our motto is Forward" Forward and Kill"
Any Jerry moving make him be still
In this war in '44
The purpose of it to see this is no more
So, we will keep pushing and doing our best
Giving the Hun no chance to rest
And soon all this will be but a memory

THE QUILT

And I'll build a real home with a gal who waits for me

The GIs always seemed to maintain their sense of humor even during the battle. The following are some excerpts taken from a letter that Mac sent to his sweetheart, Rae Wyland, whom he called "Chire" on July 21, 1944.

Did I ever tell you about Josh Slushalong from Kentucky? He says his been away so long now he almost forgot how it feels to have the good old Kentucky mud squeeze up between his toes. There's plenty of mud but when the army gave him shoes, he went and nailed them on. At that I don't think the nails went into his feet for one day he accidentally stayed in the water 2 hours and underneath several layers of clothing he took off to ring out the remains of a diaper. Says his family never did throw away old clothes, they simply put the new ones on over. I admit it did save patching. Nearly broke Josh's heart when they cut his hair, but he was grateful afterwards when he found out he had two eyes. Strangely enough he didn't need a shave. Seems like some Indians had taught him to pluck his whiskers out. Considered he'd done a hard day's work when he plucked 10 to 12 hairs out. The Indians made him give them some of his right powerful stuff. It ought to be they held a weekly barn dance in the vat in order to get all the juice out of the mash. Some of the boys really spat out some sizeable cuds to mix in with it. Josh's grandpop old Plunk they called him never did have much use for an age. He chewed a mean cud so's they say. He could hack down a tree at 20 paces and if it started to fall towards him, he always had a spare cud to spit with so's he wouldn't get hit. Josh says the skeeters are so big home that they use chicken wire to keep them out. That don't do much good though for the big ones push the little ones through so's they can open the door for them. Josh says he can always tell when there's been a hard first frost in the fall. They always leave the barn door open as soon as summer is nearly gone and sure enough when Jack Frost hits real hard why the pumpkins snap off the vine and start rolling into the barn. One year, Josh forgot to put the scarecrow up to direct traffic and the pumpkins rolled into town and sold themselves. He didn't have any trouble getting the money for them for Jim his pet crow had followed them in and after much caw, cawing had got the money......

Josh says it gets pretty hot at home. Says they have to pick the corn early else it will pop all over the fields.
Says when they do want popcorn, they just load up the shotgun with corn. Shoot it at a pair of flannels on the line and by the time the corn gets there it will be popped and ready to eat out of the legs of the flannels. The sweaty flannels salt the corn enough and a little grease in the barrel of the gun saves buttering it. One day a sudden rain cooled things off and the corn instead of popping went right through the seat of the flannels. Grandma had to get out the red paint and camouflage grandpa before he could wear them for that's all he wore. Who knows maybe will have some of Josh's vegetables over here. He dug a tater vine from underneath his thumbnail and planted it...

CHAPTER 7:
LIBERATION

The 26th Infantry had earned another battle ribbon for Normandy and soon would add another for the liberation of France. After Cobra broke through the German lines allowing the Allies to advance away from the Normandy beaches, the army pushed through a pocket at Falaise on their way to Paris. By this time, General Patton was back "in the saddle" in command of the Third army. The Allies tried to surround and trap the Germans, but a good number escaped. An estimated 10,000, lay dead and another 50,000 more were captured. There were also nearly 700 tanks and self- propelled guns wrecked or abandoned. [67]Many if not most of the dead had not yet been buried.

> *"German guns and trucks and wagons, bloated dead by the score were everywhere... A German officer sat in the rear of a limousine next to his stylish mistress, both dead from cannon shells through the chest. 'it was if,' one officer wrote, 'an avenging angel had swept the area bent on destroying all things German.'.... Troops cleansing the pocket wore gas masks to cope with what became known as the 'Falaise smell.' Corruption even seeped into Spitfire cockpits at fifteen hundred feet."[68]*

---

67 Ibid. Rick Atkinson, p.169.
68 Ibid. Rick Atkinson, p.170.

During the month of August, the army liberated the western portions of France.[69] Paris was liberated August 23-25. Between August 26 and September 11, 1944, the Allies pushed into Belgium. There was so much destruction, however, that the "GI's made puns about whether yet another town had been liberated or 'ob-liberated'." Soldiers began to chant: "End the war in '44". While the Allies ultimately aimed at Berlin, the best way to get there was to destroy Germany's industrial complex in the Ruhr valley. Two-thirds of German steel and more than half the country's coal came from the Ruhr and loss of that region would seriously compromise the Reich's ability to produce ammunition and explosives. Meanwhile, the British moved into the Netherlands between September 17-26.[70]

The first city targeted in Germany was the city of Aachen.

> "For most loyal Germans, Aachen had always seemed a city worth dying for. Thermal springs believed to have healing powers had lured first the Romans and then the Carolingians. Here Charlemagne may have been born and here certainly he died, in 814, after creating the First Reich... thirty kings and twelve queens had been anointed, crowned, and enthroned..., The cathedral also housed four relics...the apparel of the Virgin, the swaddling clothes and loincloth of Christ, and the garment John the Baptist wore at his decapitation."[71]

The 26th was assigned to attack the city.

---

69 Michael Green &James d. Brown, "Patton's Third Army in World War II", Crestline, New York, NY, 2010, p.82.
70 Ibid. Rick Atkinson, pp. 174, 222, 158. 223, 258.
71 Ibid. Rick Atkinson, p. 291.

Aachen

The bombardment of Aachen began on October 11, 1944. The allied planes dropped one hundred and sixty-two tons of bombs 10,000 artillery shells on the city for two days and then Mac's unit went in. They found a "sterile sea of rubble" with only 20.000 of the original 165,000 inhabitants. The army

---

72 Ibid. Rick Atkinson, p.290.

had learned that if you meet resistance, you knock everything down. They went in street by street, building by building, room by room, and cleared out the defenders. Tanks or tank destroyers were used to destroy buildings floor by floor, from street to attic; forcing the defenders into cellars where, if they did not surrender, were finished off with grenades. After the Italian campaign, they added a 155mm gun mounted on a tank chassis that could demolish buildings. The troops crept forward at a steady pace of fifty feet per hour. Meanwhile on ridges outside the city, the Germans bombarded the Americans with such savage fire that the 26th was forced to seek shelter during the daylight hours.[73] Mac was wounded in the ankle on October 11th which later earned him a purple heart.[74] By the time everything was over, the enemy had lost 63 of 90 panzer tanks, 12,000 Germans had been captured or killed, and 83 per cent of Aachen had been destroyed or damaged. American casualties were almost 6,000. The first German city of the war had been liberated.[75]

Mac's purple heart

73 Ibid. Rick Atkinson, pp.293-296.
74 Honorable Discharge Papers.
75 Ibid. Rick Atkinson, pp.297-300.

Casualties were mounting on both sides, 4,000 a day for the Germans, and there had been a third of a million since the Normandy landing on June 6th. The biggest issue at this point in the war for both sides was not the will to fight, but keeping the soldiers supplied with what they needed to continue the fight. Allied divisions were kept in the rear, because of insufficient means to support them. The most desperate need obviously was ammunition, which was being used up at a rate of 2 tons per minute every hour of every day. It was not just the ammunition, however, 3.5 billion pounds of food, "equivalent to 340 loaded liberty ships," were needed to carry the war through the winter. Clothing was wearing out faster than the clothing manufacturers could make them. There were so many supplies needed that entire fleets served as floating warehouses. There were rallies in key plants to boost ammunition under the slogan "Firepower for Eisenhower".[76] The only consolation was that the Germans were in just as desperate straits as the Allies.

Mac would be out of the action for a while as his ankle wound healed. Aachen was part of the Rhineland area basically between the Roer and the Rhine rivers. It was a heavily defended area and would take a long time compared to the other campaigns to complete. The campaign lasted from September 14, 1944 to March 21, 1945. It was difficult and costly; the Germans were defending their homeland. There were all sorts of problems. In the Hurtgen forest, for example, the trees were so thick that the area "neutralized the U.S. advantages in armor, artillery, airpower, and mobility." "One regiment took four days to move a mile; another needed five. By mid-October the division … had suffered 4,500 casualties to gain three thousand yards.[77] The Americans also learned from a safe found in Aachen, that the Germans had plans for demolishing dams upriver. The loss of the dams would flood the Roer valley for 20 miles or create a catastrophic wall of water to wash out everything in its path including needed bridges.[78] Over 3 months, 120,000 soldiers would be put into Hurtgen at a loss of 33,000 casualties.[79]

76 Ibid. Rick Atkinson, pp.00-302.
77 Ibid. Rick Atkinson, p.313.
78 Ibid. Rick Atkinson, p.315.
79 Ibid. Rick Atkinson, p.325.

The weather was also a factor. Of the 30 days in November, on only 2 did it not rain or snow.

> *"Radios and mine detectors shorted out, trucks bogged to the bumpers, and frozen mud made wool coats unbearably bulky. 'Men were forced to discard their overcoats because they lacked the strength to wear them,' a staff officer noted. 'There hands are so numb that they have to help one another on with their equipment.'"*[80]

Most troops were inadequately clothed. The cold winter weather created another problem, trench foot- a crippling injury to blood vessels and tissues caused by prolonged exposure to cold, wet conditions. November and December saw 23,000 men hospitalized with trench foot and other cold weather problems.[81] Men were tired or war and, on every continent, there were women who would exchange sexual favors for money or rations. The VD rate climbed especially after Paris was liberated. It was such a problem that Eisenhower had to declare "all brothels, bordellos and similar establishments" off limits.[82] Men like Mac with wives and sweethearts back home had a little more incentive to refrain from participating.

The Germans had their problems also. Their Achilles heel was oil. From 1942 to 1944 Germany generated 23 million tons of fuel while the United States produced more than 600 million tons. By the spring of 1945, heavy Allied attacks against the German oil targets reduced German output to 12 per cent. The British were also getting payback for the continuous bombings of London earlier in the war; now German cities and towns were being bombed. The bombings left 400,000 dead and 7 million homeless.[83] They were running out of supplies, ammunition, fuel, and new recruits to put into the fight. German factories were not keeping up with losses. From January through October of 1944, the Germans lost 118,000 military trucks but the factories only produced 46,000 new ones. Bombardment in the industrial

---

80 Ibid. Rick Atkinson, p.334.
81 Ibid. Rick Atkinson, pp. 338-339.
82 Ibid. Rick Atkinson, p. 401.
83 Ibid. Rick Atkinson, p.358.

Ruhr valley halved steel production. Workers were made to work sixty and seventy-two-hour work weeks. Hitler lowered the draft age to 16 and raised it to 50 to replace the 50,000 killed in action each month.[84] Hitler was getting desperate and was pushing every soldier to fight to the last man. The setting was ripe for the last-ditch all-out effort to punch through the Allied lines and recapture lost territory. He had ordered the German forces to do it once before earlier in the war and at the same place which led to the defeat of France. In his mind, he was a military genius, and he would do it again. The location was Ardennes and officially was known as the Ardennes campaign. To the GI's it was known as the battle of the Bulge. The first wave would consist of 200,000 men in twenty divisions with 2,000 artillery pieces, nearly a thousand tanks and assault guns. A second wave would follow, with five more divisions and hundreds of additional panzers.[85]

"The trial ahead would also require stupendous firepower and great gouts of blood in what became the largest battle in American History, and among the most decisive."[86]

Mac added a National Service and an army Good Conduct Medal to the other ribbons he could wear on his uniform.

---

84 Ibid. Rick Atkinson, pp. 390-39.
85 Ibid. Rick Atkinson, p. 395.
86 Ibid. Rick Atkinson, p.412.

National Service Medal   *Army Good Conduct Medal*

CHAPTER 8:
NUTS

itler ordered the Sixth Panzer army to attack and punch through the Allied lines on December 16, 1944. By this time Mac had recovered from his ankle wound and was back with the 26th. The Germans had roughly a five-to-one advantage over the U.S. forces in artillery and a three-to-one advantage in armor.[87]

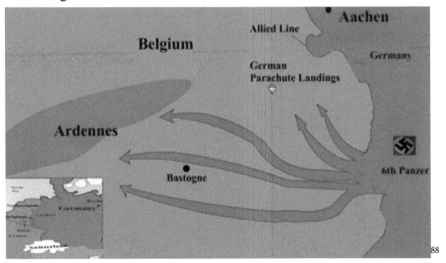

---

87 Ibid. Rick Atkinson, p.419.
88 Ibid. Rick Atkinson, p.420.

"The struggle would last for a month, embroiling more than a million men drawn from across half a continent to this haunted upland. The first act of the drama, perhaps the most decisive, played out simultaneously across three sanguinary fields scattered over sixty miles- on the American left, on the American right, and in the calamitous center."[89]

The leader of the Panzer division was a man by the name of Joachim Peiper. He had spent most of the war fighting the Russians in the east, burning villages and slaughtering civilians. His unit was known as the "Blow Torch Battalion. He would now ply his trade against the Americans and continue the atrocities. On the first day, twelve GIs who were caught sleeping were brought outside and promptly machined gunned as they tried to surrender. Another was crushed under a tank as he pleaded for mercy. Later more than a hundred prisoners were taken, when Peiper ran into an American convoy. Two panzer machine guns "chewed into the ranks of prisoners still standing with their hands raised. SS men then walked through the bloody pile and killed any they still found breathing. A dozen more GIs were found and killed. The bodies were mounded and later passing SS convoys fired into the pile for sport. Another German sergeant had eight Americans dig graves for three German soldiers and then shot them in the head. Some GIs feigning death for more than two hours rose and escaped and passed on word of the massacre. It would be passed from foxhole to foxhole up the chain of command.[90]

---

89 Ibid. Atkinson, pp. 421-422
90 Ibid. Atkinson, pp. 422-425.

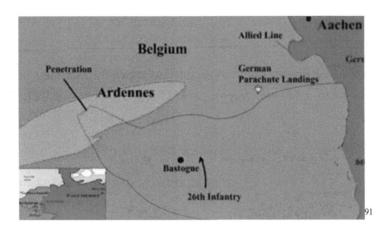

The 26th Infantry was assigned to hold the line on the southern front. The heaviest fighting was against the 26th Infantry's 2nd battalion.

> *"The 2nd battalion's right flank crumbled, and SS tanks wheeled up and down the line, crushing GIs in their foxholes."*[92]

The U.S. Sherman tanks, and the new 99mm tank destroyers fought back taking a heavy toll on the invaders and the American line held. The sixth Panzer Army reached "its high- water mark".[93] Others did not fare as well.

> *"The 110th Infantry had been annihilated, with 2,500 battle casualties. Sixty American tanks were reduced to smoking wreckage. Yet once again space had been traded for time, a few miles for forty-eight hours, and once again that bargain favored the defenders. The southern shoulder was jammed almost as effectively as the northern. Fifth Panzer Army now marched on Bastogne, true enough, but the stumbling, tardy advance by three bloodied divisions hardly resembled the blitzkrieg of Hitler's fever dream."*[94]

Among the worst was those divisions in the center of the "bulge". They were being surrounded and trapped with fire from three sides. Large numbers

91 Ibid Michael Green and James Brown, p.174.
92 Ibid. Rick Atkinson, p. 427.
93 Ibid. Rick Atkinson, p. 428.
94 Ibid. Rick Atkinson, p.432.

were ordered to smash their weapons and surrender. It was the worst defeat in the European theater.[95]

The Americans needed a counterattack to shove the Germans back through the hole they had made and "repair" the "bulge". Eisenhower looked to Patton and asked

"George, how soon can you get an attack off?"

"On December 22," Patton replied, with three divisions- the 4th Armored, the 26th, and the 80th."[96]

While Patton was getting his forces in place, the city of Bastogne was surrounded with 45,000 German soldiers. McAuliffe, the American commander, was cutoff inside with 18,000 soldiers under orders to hold at all costs. McAuliffe was given two hours to surrender or be annihilated by German artillery by the German commander, Lieutenant General Heinrich von Luttwitz. McAuliffe offered a one word now famous answer to the German general: "Nuts." It was only later that it was learned that the general was bluffing, they did not have the artillery power to make good on his threat.[97] Ammunition was getting low inside Bastogne, but luckily the skies cleared sufficiently to resupply McAuliffe by air. Patton's forces raced to aid Bastogne and destroy the German advance in the south, while Montgomery with aid of some American units was assigned to move in from the north. The first unit to reach Bastogne was the 37th Tank Battalion commanded by Lieutenant Colonel Creighton W. Abrams; Jr. Bastogne was saved.

Hitler's forces were stopped, and it was the beginning of the end for the German Reich. The gamble was costly for both sides. The bold panzer division under Peiper was reduced from 5,800 down to 770.[98] The U.S. battle losses from December 16 to January 25 were 105,000 including over 19,000 dead. Roughly one in ten U.S. combat casualties during World War II occurred in

---

95 Ibid. Rick Atkinson, p. 437.
96 Ibid. Rick Atkinson, p. 446.
97 Ibid/ Rick Atkinson, pp.455-456.
98 Ibid. Rick Atkinson, p. 462.

the bulge. A U.S. army estimate of German losses was 120.000. The Germans lost 700 armored vehicles. "After five years of war, more than four million German soldiers had been killed, wounded, or captured." The German fuel production for November and December was used in the Bulge offensive which now left hundreds of tanks on the Russian front immobilized.[99]

Mac and his 26th Infantry was in the thick of it. They helped hold the line and clear the way for the rest of Patton's forces to reach Bastogne and push the Germans back. According to a list Of Presidential Unit Citation recipients, the 26th was awarded the PCU for their participation in the Ardennes-Alsace (Battle of the Bulge) campaign. Whether this was in addition to the one recorded in Mac's discharge papers 5 August 1943 or the date on his discharge papers was wrong, is not known. It is possible the unit deserved both. They were in heavy combat in Sicily and the Bulge. The unit also added another battle ribbon for Ardennes.

---

99 Ibid. Rick Atkinson, pp. 486-490.

CHAPTER 9:
FINISH

The winter of 1945 was the worst in decades. One soldier from the 84th Division awoke with his feet" encased in a block of ice". Some GIs jerked awake by gunfire left patches of hair stuck to the icy ground. The troops were tired of war and the Fall rallying cry "Win the War in '44" changed to "Stay Alive in '45". One lieutenant in the 99th Division perhaps reflecting the sentiments of a lot of soldiers wrote:

> *"To date, I've slept on a mattress, a steel deck, a wet concrete floor with a little straw on top, dirt floors, a bed, a stretcher, on an LST, in a truck, in a foxhole, across the front seats of a jeep, in a rope hammock, in cellars, first, second, and third floors, in a pillbox, on the back window shelf of a command car, in a hayloft, on snow, and in shacks."*

Rick Atkinson reflecting on what the soldiers saw wrote:

> *"There were horrors to see, hear, smell, horrors to relive and remember because they could never be forgotten.... Everywhere we searched we found bodies, floating in the rivers, trampled on the roads, bloated in the ditches, rotting in the bunkers, pretzeled into foxholes, burned in the tanks, buried in the snow, sprawled in doorways, splattered in*

gutters, dismembered in minefields, and even literally blown up into trees."[100]

A few soldiers, less than one-half of one percent, started committing the very crimes they had come into the war to fight against. The "liberators have turned into looters, rapists, and killers."[101] The army was advancing but:

> *"'We're advancing as fast as the looting will permit,' a 29ᵗʰ Division unit in Munchen-Gladbach reported. German towns were 'processed,' houses 'liberated' from attic to cellar with everything from Leica cameras to accordions pilfered. A corps provost marshal complained of 'gangsterism' by GIs who were 'looting and bullying civilians';... Plundering MPs were known as the 'Lootwaffe;'"*[102]

The army was closing in on the Rhine River, which was broad, deep, and fast enough that it would prove a difficult obstacle to overcome. The Germans in desperation were blowing up most of the bridges across the Rhine to impede U.S. progress. The army got a lucky break, though, reaching the Remagen bridge intact. The Germans had laid explosives to blow it up, but before they could do so, a company from the 27ᵗʰ Armored Infantry Battalion raced to the bridge and eliminated the explosion threat.[103] A week later there were 8 bridges across the Rhine near Remagen and the "inner door to Germany had swung wide open, never to be shut again."[104]

The U.S. army moved eastward, Montgomery and the British and Canadian army moved from the north while the Soviet Union was moving in from the west. Germany was being crushed in between. Bombing intensified with March 1945 "the heaviest bombing month of the war: 130,000 tons."[105] The U.S. would erect 57 more bridges across the Rhine. Six thousand tanks would cross over. "The terrible swift sword was fully drawn." "No sword was swifter or more terrible than Patton's" He had an incentive; his beloved son-

---

100 Ibid. Rick Atkinson, pp. 524-525.
101 Ibid. Rick Atkinson, p.528.
102 Ibid. Rick Atkinson, p. 545.
103 Ibid. Rick Atkinson, pp.548-551.
104 Ibid. Rick Atkinson, p.555.
105 Ibid. Rick Atkinson, p.567.

in-law, Lieutenant Colonel John Knight Waters had been captured in Tunisia on Valentine's Day, 1943 at Kasserine Pass and being held along with 1,500 other American officers in a prison camp in northern Poland.[106]

Many German prisoners were taken. By mid-April the total war numbers had grown to over 1.6 million with 323,000 from the Ruhr area in April alone.[107] Mac's unit moved with the army eastward and in April, they reached Braunlage in the Goslar district of Germany on their way toward Berlin.

Somewhere on the battlefield Mac may have written the following poem.

Sentiments

I'm an awful wreck and I guess by heck a hell of a fightin' man.

My hair is turning grey what hasn't gone away but still I do the best I can.

---

106 Ibid. Rick Atkinson, pp. 568-569.
107 Ibid. Rick Atkinson, p. 585.

I may be going blind and nearly lose my mind when shells start falling everywhere.
Skeeter, flies, and fleas are busy as bees getting at me in this fresh air.
Still, I'm not the one to kick longs my heart says tick, tick.
For I know that when this war is over and Hitler's seeing Satan my girl will be waitin'
Maybe in a field of clover maybe in silk and laces ready to go certain places.
Even ready to say I do but what she may be wearing I won't be a caring.
Long she says I love you.
As this poem maybe boring and get you a snoring I'll end it the best I know
And after final victory as I sail back across the sea straight to this lass, I'll go.
Give her a hug and a great big kiss then settle down to a life of bliss.

Mac was wounded a second-time April 12th, 1945. This wound was a shrapnel wound from a rifle grenade in his left arm. An Oak Leaf Cluster was added to the purple heart received from his first wound. This time there was a newspaper article with some other wounded warriors coming back home to heal. His left arm appeared to be in a cast and heavily bandaged. Mac was not sure that wound would heal, and he would get the use of his arm back. He did though and for him the war was over. He would go home.

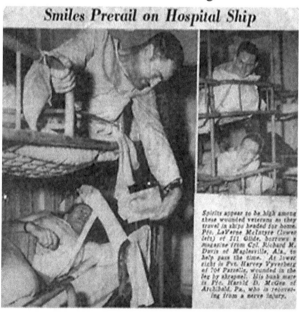

Smiles Prevail on Hospital Ship

Spirits appear to be high among these wounded veterans as they travel in ships headed for home. Pfc. LaVerne McIntyre (lower left) of III Glide, borrows a magazine from Cpl. Richard M. Davis of Maplesville, Ala., to help pass the time. At lower right is Pvt. Harvey Vyverberg of 704 Parsells, wounded in the leg by shrapnel. His bunk mate is Pfc. Harold D. McGee of Archbald, Pa., who is recovering from a nerve injury.

The 26th unit would keep on until the end of the war. Once the army was in Germany, they began to discover the unexpected. In the Thuringian village of Merkers, they found a cache of treasure horded by Hitler. There were 8,307 gold bars, 35 crates of bullion, 3,682 sacks of German currency, 80 more of foreign currency, 3,326 bags of gold coins among them 711 bags filled with U.S. $20 gold pieces, 8 bags of gold rings and a pouch of platinum bars. In other areas were valuables stolen from concentration camp victims.

> *"If these were the old free-booting days when a soldier kept his loot,' Bradley told Patton, 'you'd be the richest man in the world'".*

It was valued at half a billion dollars at that time.[108] Hitler was amassing his fortune. The army also discovered the horrors of Hitler's concentration camps. The first to be liberated was Buchenwald.

> *"We passed through the stockade. More than 3,200 naked, emaciated bodies had been flung into shallow graves. Others lay in the street where they had fallen... A guard showed us how the blood had congealed in the coarse black scabs where the starving prisoners had torn out the entrails of the dead for food."[109]*

Mac's unit liberated the Gusen concentration camp and saw the horrors inflicted by the Nazi's under Hitler firsthand.[110] Mac was probably grateful he did not have to see that horror firsthand.

> *"For the liberators, this great floodtide of misery was unnerving."*

> *"Soldiers who in years of combat had seen things no man should ever see now gawked in disbelief at the iniquities confronting them."*

> *"..the Bergen-Belsen camp, fifty miles south of Hamburg. 'We came into a smell of ordure-like the smell of a monkey camp,' a British intelligence officer reported, and a 'strange simian throng' greeted them at the gates. Over forty thousand men, women, and children*

---

108 Ibid. Rick Atkinson, pp. 587-588.
109 Ibid. Rick Atkinson, p. 589.
110 Wikipedia, 26th Infantry Division (United States)

jammed a compound designed for eight thousand; since January they had survived on watery soup, fourteen ounces of rye bread a day, and a kind of beet called mangel-wurzel, normally used as livestock feed. But the past four days they had received neither food nor water and were reduced to eating the hearts, livers, and kidneys of the dead."

"The living looked like 'polished skeletons"[111]

Hitler was exterminating the Jews and any others he deemed undesirable. It is common knowledge that 6 million Jews died in the death camps. He added insult to everything by stealing everything they owned. Victory in Europe was celebrated on May 8, 1945.

"Twelve years and four months after it began, the Thousand-Year Reich had ended. Humanity would require decades, perhaps centuries, to parse the regime's inhumanity, and to comprehend how a narcissistic beerhall demagogue had wrecked a nation, a continent, and nearly a world."[112]

Mac came home and indulged his biggest peacetime passion, playing bridge. He was rather good at it too as the following newspaper clippings will attest.

---

111 Ibid. Rick Atkinson, pp. 600-601/
112 Ibid. Rick Atkinson, pp.614-615.

Later Japan surrendered and the war was officially over September 2, 1945. The country was jubilant. Armed service veterans were well received when they returned. They had rid the world of Hitler and his Nazi war machine in Europe and the Japanize menace in the Pacific. America was proud of its heroes and showed it. It was a time of hope. It was time of joyful expectation that the future was very bright and promising. It was time to "suck it up" and bury the memories of war. It was time to marry that woman that had waited for him to come home.

CHAPTER 10:
HOPE

Laverne and Rae were married on September 11, 1945 in an alcove at Lake Avenue Baptist Church. The reception was held at Laverne's brother Walt and his wife Louise's house. They spent the first night in Hotel Seneca on Clinton Avenue in Rochester, New York. From there, they went on to the 1,000 Islands for a honeymoon. Mac wore his uniform at lot and was treated like a returning hero and given a lot of breaks.

Beginning Rear Left: First 3 Unknown, Louse and Husband Walt, Verna Mae, Laverne, Rae, Next couple unknown, Rayma (Roy's first wife), Roy, Effie, Effie's son Bud. Continuing around the table: Unknown lady, Roy junior, Helen (Walt and Louise's daughter), Marilyn (Roy's daughter), Charlie and Terry (Walt and Louise's sons)

The following poem was found among Mac's things. Whether he wrote it or not is not known but it may very well have expressed his feelings about having children and raising a family.

Boy or Girl

Some folks pray for a boy, and some for a golden-haired little girl to come
Some claim to think there is more joy wrapped up in the smile of a little boy
While others pretend that the silky curls and plump, pink cheeks of the little girls
Bring more of bliss to the old home place then a small boys little freckled face

Now which is better, I couldn't say if the Lord should ask me to choose today
If He should put in a call for me and say: "Now what shall your order be
A boy or girl? I have both in store—Which of the two are you waiting for?"
I'd say with one of my broadest grins "send either one, if it can't be twins."

I've heard it said, to some people's shame, they cried with grief when a small boy came
For they wanted a girl, and some folks I know who wanted a boy, just took on so
When a girl was sent. But it seems to me that mothers and fathers should happy be
To think, when the Stork has come and gone that the Lord would trust them with either one

Boy or girl? There can be no choice; there is something lovely in either voice
And all that I ask of the Lord to do is see that the mother comes safely through
And guard the baby and have it well, with a perfect form and a healthy yell,
And a pair of eyes and a shock of hair then boy or girl its dad won't care.

David Philip was born just about nine months later and arrived just 2 days before Laverne's birthday on June 2, 1946. Rae was Jewish and perhaps that influenced the name. King David was a prominent figure in Jewish history. Her father's name was Phillips Wyland and that probably was the inspiration for the middle name. Apparently, Rae and Laverne liked names beginning with D and named their second child Dennis Allen McIntyre. He was born almost a year and half later November 6, 1947. His middle name reflected the Allen maiden name of Laverne's mother Verna. Douglas Walter McIntyre was born on January 26th, 1949 completing the clan. His middle name came from Laverne's second oldest brother Walter. Laverne and Rae now had their hands full with 3 children less than 3 years old. I guess Laverne may have been thinking that he had better get started with a family. After all he was almost 36 when David was born, and his father had died at age 42.

Rae's Jewish heritage may have affected her parenting of her first-born son. For whatever reason, maybe she remembered the story of Samson in the Bible, she did not cut David's hair for at least the first year and a half. There is a picture of him with his brother Denny with shoulder length hair. All three of the boys had brown hair and light blue eyes. Denny is especially fond of telling David later that he was a cute kid as a baby. Then he always added afterward: "What the heck happened". Brotherly love!

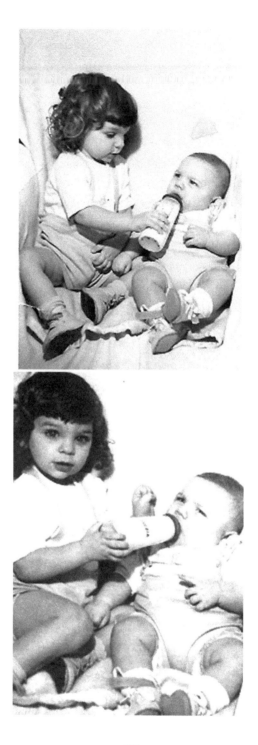

Rae was well established, but Laverne now had to find work. He did not have as much education as Rae. Laverne worked with his hands. Eventually, he became a machinist. At the end of the war, however, Rae was the major bread winner.

David had several childhood memories growing up in the McIntyre home. The reader should keep in mind that these are the memories of a child of around 4 years old. These memories were real in his mind. He believed that they were all true. Probably the earliest memory was living in a two-story gray house with a driveway along the side of the house and a detached garage in the back. He did not remember much about the inside of the house, probably because the boys played mostly outside. While there were some steps up to a front entrance, it seems they always entered the house from the rear. The rear had steps also and he remembered a tree to the left side. To him the tree was huge, and he was especially proud one day when he climbed almost to the top of that tree. That "tree" was probably more like a bush, and he climbed just high enough to be eye to eye with his mom. Even so he was praised for the accomplishment. There were some older kids in the neighborhood and the brothers became the audience for their plays. The running board on Rae and Laverne's car served as bench seats. They had to stay and see the entire performance and respond with the appropriate enthusiasm.

Laverne and Rae's first house

Not all memories were good. Along the side of the house was a milk box that was used for home milk deliveries. One day, while David was inside the hallway at the top of the steps, he caught and pinched his finger in that milk box. It Hurt! His mom came out when she heard him crying. She seemed to take the pain away and make it all better. The pain would probably have subsided on its own and Rae really did not do much more than give him comfort but to David she was a miracle worker. He felt loved.

Laverne and Rae acquired a house in Spencerport at 2930 Nichols Street. It was a modest two-bedroom one bath house. David remembered the floor plan as in the following diagram.

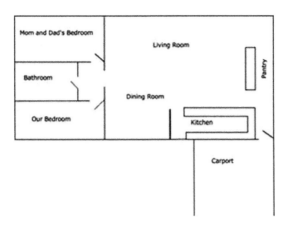

The house had a big lawn and David remembers his mom sitting down on the grass with him and teaching him how to find four-leaf clovers in the grass. They did not find many, but they got excited when they did. The house had a driveway that ran up a slight hill and curved around toward the house. He also remembers that they had a dog named Pepe. He was a black and white shepherd, the kind you see in movies herding sheep. They loved that dog and remembered hugging and playing with him. They were the perfect post war family.

When David was about 4, Laverne and Rae and the boys took a vacation trip to the Thousand Islands in New York State, Laverne's favorite vacation spot. The weather was relatively warm that summer of 1950. David remembers a ferry pontoon boat with an isle down the center and bench seats on either side of the isle. Rae and the boys sat toward the back. A nice lady made a nice comment to Rae about her boys and asked if she could give them some gum. Rae said yes and the boys got the treat. David also remembers a seaplane ride. Rae and the three boys sat in the back. Laverne sat in the seat next to the pilot. The boys did not sit very high, so they couldn't see much, they just felt the motion.

There was another time also that same summer in which Rae and Mac were sitting on a blanket at the beach, probably Charlotte on Lake Ontario. Denny and David were playing around them. Someone videoed that scene.

On another occasion, again probably during the warm months of 1950, Rae played with her three boys. It had to be the summer of 1950 because none of the boys were wearing jackets and Doug was walking, even running a little. Rae wore a blouse and a skirt and squatted down as her three boys took turns running away from her and then back to her. They each pounced on her all the while laughing as they did it. Many years later the boys' Aunt Effie and her husband Russ showed David and his wife Jan the videos of those summer events. The videos were never passed on to Laverne or his boys when Russ and Effie died. Dennis never remembers his mother, but knew she loved him. The super eight movies he viewed with Aunt Effie showed how much she enjoyed frolicking on the floor with all three of her sons. The love he felt quickly left him when she died.

Artist Natasha Fisch

One of David's last memories probably occurred later that same year around the beginning of December. It was colder. The three boys were ushered through a hall in a building into a smaller room where they sang the song: "I Saw Mommy Kissing Santa Claus". David and Denny carried the tune and Doug tried his best to keep up. The room was part of a recording studio for a radio program and the boys were apparently part of a kids Christmas program. Kids have a way of stealing the show even when they make mistakes. Rae was not with them; perhaps she was listening intently, though, to her boys perform.

They were happy. They were totally unprepared for what was about to happen next.

CHAPTER 11:
DISASTER

It was December 10, 1950. The house was full of people. Something was up. David did not remember seeing his mom for days. Then someone gathered the boys and ushered them into Rae and Laverne's bedroom. They were positioned next to the foot of her bed so she could see them clearly. She was lying there, and David remembers that she looked very white. Laverne was on the other side of the bed with his hands folded in front of him and he was looking down. There was sadness in the room. There was a heaviness, a foreboding in the air. It was something a four-and-a- half-year-old boy could feel but could not describe. Rae reached out with her right arm toward her boys but could not raise it high. She was too weak. She may have been trying to beckon them to come closer so she could hug them. She tried to say something but all that came out was I..I..I.

Artist Natasha Fisch

The boys did not stay long in the room. They were ushered out into the living room. Rae was taken out and taken to the Strong Memorial hospital. It was sometime later that David overheard an adult say that she had died on the way there. The boys never saw their mom again.

Rae was gone. As children, the boys were totally unaware that she had been fighting breast cancer. She had both breasts removed but that did not stop the disease. She had not done well with the surgery. She did not heal well. Back then, when a doctor told you that you had cancer, that was a death sentence. The best they could do was estimate about how long you had. That struggle may well have caused Rae to think about her eternal destiny. Many years later Grandma Verna told David that she had converted from her Jewish faith. David and his brothers have a hope that the conversion meant she accepted Christ as her Savior. One day they will be reunited with their mom in heaven. Laverne did not share much about her struggle with his boys. He would tear up whenever the subject was brought up. She was the love of his life and that time was very painful to him.

When people are told that they only have so long to live, priorities change. Vacations are taken to provide some happy memories for everyone. That may explain some of the memories that David had that may have occurred the summer before. He did not have a clue what all this meant. His little brain was trying to process it. Denny and Doug were too young to remember it. David missed his mom. Seventy years later he still does. Denny and Doug felt it too but being so young they could not express why they felt as they did. Many years later as an adult, Denny wrote a book called "A Legacy of Love". In it he expressed the cry of his heart that may have stemmed from the loss of mom:

> *"I never knew my mom as she passed shortly after I turned three. Dave remembers her for a short time. ... Sometimes I wish I could have known her even for that brief period to formulate something to remember her by. About fifty years later, I would have a counselor tell me what I must have felt at the time of her death. The sudden loss of affection, her gentle voice, and all those things that emulate love towards me were suddenly gone. A scared little boy was screaming 'Come back.'"* [113]

Rae was pronounced dead on arrival at Strong Memorial Hospital in Rochester New York on December 10, 1950. She was buried in Mt. Hope Cemetery.

---

113 Dennis McIntyre, "Legacy of Love", Tate Publishing & Enterprises, LLC, 2008, pp. 28-29.

CHAPTER 12:
AFTERMATH

The next years were difficult ones. Laverne loved his boys, but he was a quiet man that did not exhibit a great deal of emotion. There were not a lot of hugs and no kisses. He had to work. He had to suppress his grief and keep going, another war to fight. This time the enemy was unseen and not so easily defined. He started to develop a deep-seated anger that stayed with him all the rest of his life. He was angry at God for not saving this gal, that had waited for him. After all, she had converted from Judaism to Christianity. They were attending a Baptist church at the time, apparently trying to draw closer to God. Why then would a good God allow such a terrible thing happen and leave him with three small boys to care for all alone. He internalized his struggle and just plowed forward as best he could. For his three sons, though, it meant that they were not going to get a whole lot of outward affection from their dad.

God was there all along. He had not abandoned the boys. God does not always answer prayers in the way we think He should. He is in the healing business and he healed their Rae. He just did it after she passed on. Now He would work all the events, experiences, and situations to make each of the boys His own special creation. He would work on Laverne as well; it would just be a lot longer process requiring a lot of Godly patience. David can look back now and see God's hand in his life. Of course, as a 4-year-old boy, he understood none of it. He just missed his mother, and his dad was not a lot of comfort.

The boys stayed with Grandma and Aunt Effie for a time. They slept upstairs in the sewing room. They did not stay long though, probably just long enough for Laverne to make other arrangements. Laverne expressed some anger toward his mother and sister about it that they did not help more. They had their reasons. Effie's son Bud may have been one of them. He was about 17 at the time. He was a big boy and became a big man physically and probably a real handful as a teenager. Bud did have some trouble with the law. There was also more than one woman and at least 6 kids. He was better as he grew older. When Laverne needed help, though, he was a serious problem to Effie and a bad influence. God may have decided it would be better for the boys not to live with Effie.

David and Dennis also remember a woman named Faye. Faye came to live and take care of the boys in that same house on Nichols Street in Spencerport. The boys got on her nerves at times. Both boys remember her breaking supposedly unbreakable plates over their heads during those outbursts. The three boys were probably just being boys and as boys can get loud, roughhouse a bit, and may not exactly listen to authority. Anyone taking care of boys like that can reach the end of their patience. The boys probably did not deserve being hit over the head with the plates though. The relationship between Laverne and Faye was more economic. She apparently had a young daughter and needed support and Laverne needed someone to take care of his boys while he worked. That situation did not last long. Faye was frustrated with the boys. Also, Laverne did not earn enough to pay all the bills and keep the house. When Laverne and Rae married, there were two incomes. Rae was as an established optical designer and likely earned more than Mac. Now he had to shoulder it all. Laverne had no choice but to put the boys into the foster care system.

The boys and possibly Faye's daughter

It was a daunting job for the foster care system. Sometimes they have trouble finding homes for a single child. Now they would have to find a home that would take all three of them. From the start, the system worked awfully hard to keep them altogether. There were a few homes with a short stay. David's first year in school was completed in three different institutions. Fortunately, he liked school and was able to keep up. The boys stayed a little longer with a young couple that had a boy of their own. They treated the boys well enough, but they did have a manikin in a closet in the garage. Denny was really scared by that manikin and being in dark places in general, so he has some frightening memories. He thinks he was mistreated by being placed in a dark closet (or even with that manikin). To him the foster homes began with bitter memories. His heart was filled with the thought, "Doesn't anyone love me?" The manikin on the shelf was so frightening to him, that he beat the bottom of the door and cried until passing out. He thought the manikin was a mummy soon to come back to life. Between the ages of three and six, unhealthy demons would take their residence inside him. Three years of a loving mother's love, followed by three years of agony, had a tremendous effect on Dennis. He longed for the life he had during the first three years.

For the most part, David remembered them as trying to do the best they could. When the boys got sick, they cared for them. David just sensed that that he and his brothers were temporary boarders. They had a son. He knew the difference between a babysitter and a parent. As far as he could tell, that woman was a good person who really did care, but the boys were not hers. The boys were a job, a temporary assignment. She tried to do the job to the best of her ability, but I think God knew the boys needed a little bit more. They needed a mother.

The boys were about 8, 7 and 5 years old when they were transferred to another foster home. It was a farm at 1842 Plank Road in Webster, New York owned by Robert and Florence Harris. The Harris farm offered great relief. They were an older couple. They had raised two children of their own now married and one lived on one side of their 54-acre farm. They even had a grandchild which put them approaching 60 when the boys came to live with them. They also already had three foster children in their care, two older teenage girls named Nancy and Patti-Ann and one younger boy about Doug's age named Marty. They already had a full plate. They had a farm to take care of. Mr. Harris had several cows which he milked every day. He had chickens, a horse, and at times even a pig or two. He would get up at five in the morning and milk the cows and then go to work at a regular job like everyone else. When he came back home, the cows had to be milked again and chickens and pigs fed. Only then, could he have supper and relax. Oh, yes periodically he planted alfalfa and corn for the cows and every year harvested those crops. Mrs. Harris, besides taking care of a big old farmhouse and had a dog kennel. They were also providing a home for one of their mother's as well. I think they not only had a full plate; it was already loaded to the brim! God had to have touched their hearts to take on three more.

That is what they did. The first day the boys met them, and they introduced themselves, Mrs. Harris told them one thing that David never forgot. She said you do not have a mother; you call me mom. Mr. Harris told them that they had a dad but not a grandfather. He told the boys to call him grandpa. In one day, God, had brought the boys another mom and now a grandfather as well. They did their absolute best to be both of those to the boys all the while they were there.

Their home was a big old country farmhouse. Everyone always entered the house from the back into a hallway which passed by a staircase leading up to an attic and a large room. That room became the boy's bedroom. It easily handled 3 beds, 3 dressers, and still left plenty of floor space for anything else they might want to have in the room. Dennis and David slept on either side of a window at one end and Doug's bed was on the other side of the room. In the hallway past the steps leading to the attic, was another door that led down to the cellar. Beyond that door, was the entrance into the big country kitchen complete with a large pantry next to the entrance. Passing through the kitchen was a large dining room with a large dining room table. Nine would eat supper every night and enjoy Sunday dinners worthy of a Thanksgiving feast every week. On the left side, was a door leading out to a small front porch. Diagonally across from the kitchen entrance was a single bathroom for the house. Straight through the dining room was the living room. On the other side of the living room was a small bedroom where grandma slept. On the back of the living room to the right, was a door leading into a master bedroom. In the dining room between the living room entrance and the bathroom was another staircase, that accessed three more bedrooms. At the top of the steps on the left, was a larger master bedroom sized room, where Nancy slept. Patti-Ann and Marty slept in two smaller rooms, one on the right at the top of the stairs and one straight ahead. It had to have been an adjustment to now share the house and two parent figures with three new young strangers. How did God prepare Mr. and Mrs. Harris for the new arrivals? Whatever was said and done, worked. They felt accepted by all in house.

It was good on that farm. The boys had chores to do to be sure and they balked at them a bit, but they learned. David had to water the cows every day and feed the chickens. They took turns doing the dishes after supper. Every Saturday they had to dust the furniture. They also helped with the harvest, helping pickup and put the bales of hay in the barn. There was also a bonus from that. At times, some of the bales would break and that hay was piled up below the stacked bales in the barn. The boys had a lot of fun jumping off the stacked bales into that loose hay. That could have been dangerous, but God was watching out for them even then. One day David jumped and landed in the hay only to look over at a pitchfork with the tongs up near him. There was also that rope swing in the middle of the barn. Oh yes, there was also a nice swing hanging from a large pine tree in the front yard as well. The boys climbed things, made things out of wood they found, and played cowboys and Indians with makeshift bows and arrows. They created a barrage cannon by sticking crab apples on the branch tips of a young tree, then bending it down, and letting it spring back up hurling the apples at an unseen enemy. They rode the cows and when the docile animals did not move fast enough, they twisted their tails to get them to move faster. They were being boys and God was watching out for them. They made airplane swings and flew their fighter planes swinging over the fence. When summer came, they gorged themselves on berries on the fence rows, black cherries from several trees, and some apples in the apple orchard. Life was good and fun. Nobody got hurt.

They also learned some discipline as well. They learned it from the assigned chores. Grandpa Harris made sure that they understood that backtalking an adult was totally unacceptable. It only took one backhand for David to learn that lesson. There were also times when discipline had to be administered in the form of lost privileges when there was wrongdoing. It was always administered fairly and without anger. David remembers one occasion in which he had done something wrong in the morning. Grandpa Harris set the punishment at the loss of television privileges for that evening. When evening came, the others went into the living room to watch Howdy Doody, but David sat on a chair in the dining room and did not go in. The others asked if he was going to join them.

David said no, that was his punishment for his earlier infraction. Grandpa was in the bathroom and heard David's answer. He came out and told him to go on in and watch the program. Grandpa Harris knew that David had learned his lesson. David never forgot that and thanked God, Grandpa, and mom for the discipline lessons.

Nancy and Patti-Ann loved to ride the black horse named Beauty that also lived on the farm. The horse was docile enough to ride, but first you had to catch her. That took some doing. They would tie several pieces of binding twine together to create a longer rope and then several of them would hold the rope between them to corner Beauty in the pasture. Beauty was afraid of the electric fences around most of the fields. If she could see an opening around the rope fence, she would run but when she was finally closed off in a corner, she would give up and accept the halter. After that she obeyed nicely. David and Denny both liked to ride Beauty.

The boys learned the rudiments of electricity on that farm. If you touched the fence while grounded, you got a shock. It would hurt but would not do any real damage. It was kind of like getting shocked on a doorknob on a dry day. The boys got shocked quite a bit walking into the fence or trying to crawl under it. They learned though that if you wore sneakers you were no longer grounded, and you could touch the fence without being shocked. One day David thinking to show how brave he was grabbed the fence with both hands. Boy, was he surprised when he got shocked. He decided there was more to be learned about this electricity thing. Grandpa taught another lesson another day. He told two of the boys to grab the fence with one hand with their sneakers on. No shock. Then he simultaneously grabbed them both. They got set on their butts and everyone burst out laughing. Some of these events may have generated an interest in science and how and why things worked. Later, all 3 boys pursued science and engineering careers.

Occasionally, Mr. Harris would come home with a large cooler full of ice cream. He would pick up the about to be outdated treats and everyone would sort through to find the good stuff, which went into the freezer. The rest was fed to the pigs. On those days, everyone would gorge themselves with ice cream. The boys loved to eat cheerio ice cream bars when the barrel of treats arrived with Mr. Harris.

Summer, fall, winter, spring, there was always something to look forward to. Summer meant no school but also was a time to harvest the hay and corn for silage. Fruits and vegetables ripened, and they enjoyed the fresh corn on the cob, the apples, and oh yes, those black cherries. The boys would rig a wagon with some of the baling twine so that one end of the twine was held by someone sitting in the wagon, like reigns on a chariot. The twine was then passed through the wagon handle and wrapped around the waist of another boy. The one in front would then run around the oval driveway as fast as he could and drag the wagon behind him. It was a makeshift chariot race! That team always won. Imaginations went wild at times. They made their own toys. Some wood and carboard became a fort. A sapling and string became a bow and arrow. Climbing up the outside of the silo was like scaling a mountain (which they were not supposed to do). They had fun and did not need fancy toys to do it. Everyone enjoyed the color changes in fall and the holiday season. In winter, they enjoyed the snow. The back ponds would freeze over, and they learned that they could slide well across the ice on just their boots or with a running start on a sled. When spring came, it was plowing time. They helped Grandpa clear some of the fields of the larger rocks. He dragged a large, wooded sled behind the tractor, and they piled the bigger rocks we found on it. They were then tossed in the fence row. At times, the boys even got to drive the tractor. David loved to explore the woods for the first signs of life growing. He would search and find jack-in-the-pulpit flowers and bring back a handful to mom. She would always say something nice and how much she appreciated them.

jack-in-the-pulpit flowers

God was working through the Harris's. Mrs. Harris also was concerned about the boy's spiritual life as well. She and grandpa were devout Christians. She took them to church at Webster Baptist church every Sunday. There they learned the Bible stories. They were introduced to Noah, Abraham, Moses, and of course, Jesus. They memorized some of the Scripture. David remembers specifically learning the 23rd Psalm by heart. He gained a healthy respect for the Bible and he instinctively knew that the Bible was true. God existed, and this book needed to be reverenced. In 1956, Webster Baptist Church gave David his own King James Bible. He had it for over 60 years and only recently let it go, because it was falling apart. Later, when he would go to the movies like the Ten Commandments or Samson and Delila, he would find the stories in the Bible, so he could read the original true story. God was planting seeds. They may not have harvested until much later, but He still was planting seeds.

The boys were growing up. David had a setback, though, they made him wear shorts during the summer months. He was terribly upset at that. He did not want to wear those "little boy pants." Didn't they know he was a big boy now. It is kind of funny to think about it now because today David practically lives in shorts in the warm Florida climate. He finally got over it. He started to love reading especially the novels by Charles Dickens and Mark Twain. He imagined that he was Oliver Twist or Huck Finn and became engrossed in the adventures. He would devour the novels. He loved school and tried to do well. He started to learn how to play the cello as part of a special music program. He was home.

The boy's father Laverne was not out of the picture during these times. He came to visit about every other weekend. He spent time with them, but Laverne being Laverne was just not that communicative. David does not remember his dad saying I love you nor does he remember being hugged. Laverne loved his boys; they just had to read between the lines. One time, for example, he came out to the farm near David's birthday in June bringing him a brand-new bike. The boys were up the lane in the back part of the farm when he arrived. He did not wait for them to come back. Instead, he rode the bike up the lane to meet them. He was excited to give David that bike and somehow, David knew he did it because he loved him. Laverne could not give all of them bikes. For a time, David's bike became a community bike and they all learned how ride on it. Later it was exclusively David's.

Still, Denny's favorite memories during those formidable years were each time Laverne came to visit. He hoped that the next visit would be for good, and Laverne would take three boys to live with him. The Harris family had many positive effects, but Dennis never felt they were his parents. He remembers one day, when a rattlesnake was ready to strike a few feet away. Dennis stopped abruptly and watched the snake coil tightly. Somehow, he was able to run back to tell Mr. Harris, who came with a pitchfork to destroy it. After the snake's head was cut off, Dennis still thought it would be dangerous, as the rattle kept going long into the night. On another occasion Mr. Harris cut off the head of a snake and a small toad leaped out. The lump in the snake's neck must have been the toad's recent home. It was an amazing sight to see that the toad escaped, seemingly unharmed. Sunday dinners at the Harris farm were also a welcomed time yet being with Laverne meant everything.

Laverne and the boys

After a couple of years, it seemed Laverne started taking the boys for the weekend rather than just visiting. There also was a new lady in his life, Lena Siegel. Unbeknownst to the boys, he was preparing them to come back to live with him. That is the goal of the foster care system, to restore the family whenever possible. They advised Laverne on the best way to do it. The weekend away from the farm was pleasant enough. The boys did some different things that maybe they would not have done on the farm like go the beach or maybe fishing, one of Laverne's favorite pastimes. He had an apartment at the time with two bedrooms. The three boys slept in one bedroom in a full-sized bed.

Denny and David slept at the head and Doug at the foot of the bed. Laverne slept in the other bedroom and Lena had her own apartment. It was preparation for what was to come next.

Let me to take a moment here in the story to view things from a foster parent's point of view. To be sure, I have never been a foster parent, only a parent. As a parent, you love your kids. A good foster parent, that really is doing the job well, will love and bond to those foster children even knowing that someday they must give them up. If the goal is restoration, they cannot escape that event. As a parent, I cannot fathom giving up my kids. Once bonded to them, you cannot unbind. Mr. and Mrs. Harris knew from the start that eventually they would likely leave. They chose to take the boys and love them anyway. They knew there would be pain in separating. They just trusted God to take them through it when the time came.

It came about three years later.

CHAPTER 13:
RESTORATION

Lena Siegel was born on April 12, 1909, to a Jewish couple, Hyman and Ida Siegal. She was the second born of 4 siblings. Joseph was the oldest, then Lena, then Marion and finally the youngest Charles. According to Marion, Lena was a talented musician. She played the piano and was considering attending a school of music, possibly the well-known Eastman School of Music. Apparently, that did not happen, but she always retained the ability to play the piano. Laverne may have met her through Marion. Laverne was a machinist by trade. Marion was married to Bob Chapman and at some point, Bob and Laverne started working together at the same small machinist shop, Genesee Machine Builders. Not all Lena's early life is known but apparently, she went through some rough times and was not able to have children. She started dating Laverne and spending time with the boys. She was to say later, that she saw them as three little men and her heart went out to them.

4/19.3/

Lena   *Marion and Lena*

Laverne married Lena on February 18, 1956. They were married by a Justice of the Peace in Niagara Falls, New York. The boys did not immediately go and live with their father. Laverne had a lot of financial problems, even including a bankruptcy. Lena was good for him that way. She was very frugal, as are many Jewish people. She got him back on track. They even moved to a house in Greece, a suburb of Rochester, New York. It is not known if they purchased it or just rented, but Laverne certainly treated it like it was his. It was a modest house on Brayton Road, with a one-car garage. The front entrance opened into the living room. At one corner of the living room was a staircase leading up to a large room, that eventually became the boy's bedroom. On the opposite side of the living room to the staircase was a short hallway with a door on the left leading to the cellar and a door on the right leading out to the garage. Beyond the hallway was the kitchen. At the end of the kitchen was short hallway on the right leading to a bedroom, a bathroom, and a den.

Laverne and Lena   *House on Brayton Road*

It was 1957. David was 11 when the boys went back to live with their father, and he was not happy! The Harris farm was his home. He had put down an anchor there. If that was now gone then all the security was gone. He was not just unhappy, he was mad! Laverne and Lena had been advised by the Foster care worker assigned to the case, that this might happen and why. Laverne had an explosive temper at times, but David does not remember him blasting him for his rebellion. He and Lena seemed to take it calmly. They just let it be known that the boys were not going back to the farm.

Lena who was a couple of years older than Laverne, and having never had any children of her own, she did not have a lot of experience raising children. Taking on 3 boys, one of whom was not happy at the prospect was extremely difficult. It would be on-the- job training. Mistakes were made, but the biggest problem was David. He absolutely hated leaving the only security he had ever had, the farm. That was his home not this new arrangement. He started school again and that helped some because he liked school. Laverne and Lena also allowed him to continue learning to play the cello which he had started at the Webster school while on the farm. That did not last too long, though, one day some bully neighborhood kids pushed him down while he was walking home with a cello supplied by the school. The cello broke. Laverne had to pay for it and that was the end of the cello lessons. David was miserable. He missed his home.

When David was 12, he decided to do something about it. He got on his bike one Saturday and headed toward the farm. He had to ride completely across town to the town of Webster some 20 or more miles away. He remembered the route. He also remembered how to navigate to the farm from the town. The Webster school bus traveled it every day while the boys lived on the farm and Mrs. Harris drove the route every Sunday. It was not easy. He had never ridden that far before and there were some steep hills to negotiate. Going down was fun. He probably reached some speeds that would have scared a parent to death. Going up the other side though was drudgery. He was determined to make it, and finally did that afternoon. Mom and Grandpa seemed glad to see him and took him in. He was old enough to realize, however, that they had an obligation to contact Laverne and Lena. Mr. Harris called them but also told them that they would keep David there that night and bring him back in the morning. David got to see them all. They fed him and then the best part, he got to sleep in his old bed that night. He was home. He also knew that he had to leave. He was more ready to accept the transition, because he had just proven that his anchor was still there. They still cared about him. He was still welcome and somehow that calmed him. He knew he was in trouble when he got back, so he was not in any hurry to return. Finally, they made the trip. When David got out of the car, he just knew he was in for it. Laverne and Lena though, just did not react. He did not get a spanking or a severe talking to; they just seemed happy to have him back. They thanked Mr. Harris for returning him. He left and David went upstairs to the bedroom for a while and that was that. David never ran away again.

Lena and the boys

Over time, Lena assumed the role of the boy's mother. They even called her mom. For Doug, she was the only mom that he ever remembers. She did all the usual household duties while Laverne went to work to earn a living. She even drove the boys to church on Sundays as they had become accustomed to on the farm. She was Jewish though and did not attend herself nor did Laverne. He was still mad at God for not saving the boy's birth mother. It did not take long for the boys to drop out of church. After all, if parents did not see the need to attend, why should they.

Lena loved the boys. She, like Laverne, was not into hugs and kisses, at least not back then. They also did not praise. Thus, the boys spent more time away from home then at home. They made friends with some of the neighborhood kids and played at their house or in local fields and woods. One of those was Ed, a boy David's age that lived a few houses up the street. His house became a second home. He had three brothers and a sister. They all lived in a small two-bedroom house. If David happened to be over there at suppertime, they just made a plate up for him as well. That took a bit of doing too because there was not very much room around that kitchen table. Ed's mother also could not bring herself to throw away anything that she might need later so the house was packed everywhere with those items. The house was way too small for the size of their family. Later, they raised the roof and added a second floor with a couple of other rooms. That helped. Ed and David explored, went fishing, and joined the boy scouts together. There were several camping trips some more memorable than others. Like the time they camped out during winter and the temperature dropped to a minus 8 degrees. Ed and David had to share the same sleeping bag with a blanket to keep warm. The following morning, David could not put his boots on because they were frozen at an angle. He had to hobble over to the fire to thaw them out first. Another time they camped out on Navy Island in the Niagara River above Niagara Falls. It was May and that river was cold, but the weather was warm. Many of the boys wanted to go swimming but had not thought to bring swimsuits. David did have his. The other boys just stripped naked and went in anyway; after all there was no one around. Well, almost, a boat showed up with several girls. The boys ducked down in the icy water. The girls seemed absolutely delighted to watch as those boys shivered and turned blue. Laverne never went on any of those camping trips; he had enough camping in World War II. He did help collect papers to earn money for the scouts, however.

Laverne did take the boys fishing at times. It was one of the things he really liked to do. After winter was over when the weather grew warm, he would take them trout fishing in a stocked stream not too far away. Sometimes they would get lucky and land a few. That was fun. He also had some favorite spots along the ponds adjoining Lake Ontario. They were more like lakes and fed into the Lake Ontario. In the warmer spring and summer months, fish would come into spawn and fishing would improve. Laverne loved to go there when the perch were running. They were decent size and very tasty eating. They would stake out a spot but invariably as soon as their dad caught one, he had three sons all trying to steal his spot. He got aggravated with them at that and told them to find their own place to fish. The boys would move over maybe two feet. Any fish they caught would be scaled, beheaded, and gutted and brought home to Lena to cook. She would pan fry them and serve them up. They would devour them watching out for the bones. There were hardly even bones left when Lena finished. How she loved fish. Laverne would take a week off during the summer for vacation. One of his most favorite places was the Thousand Islands. He would rent a cabin on the river with a dock and some rowboats. He and the boys would fish for pan fish and maybe some bass. Anything they caught was eaten. Sometimes they would try to fish from the dock which one day turned out to be hazardous. One day, Dennis fell in cast. Lena grabbed him by the hair and pulled him out. This was noteworthy, because all the boys had brush cuts. One summer, Uncle Bob, Aunt Marion, Suzy, and Karen joined them, and they all went to Echo Lake in the North-East corner of New York State. That was a beautiful lake with a promise of catching some nice bass and pike along with the normal pan fish. Denny seemed to have the luck though. He would fish on one side of the boat with barely enough worm on to cover the hook while Uncle Bob or his father would fish on the other side with fancier tackle and bait. He would catch a big bass. If they switched sides, he would do it again on the other side. He always seemed to be the luckiest kid alive.

Laverne and the boys

Laverne would take the boys to the movies or rather send them. He would hand them a dollar to pay for a matinee which was only about twenty-five cents back then and the remainder they could spend on candy. While they were in the movie, he would go to the pool hall down the street and play billiards. When the boys were done, they would walk to the pool hall and watch him finish up his last game and then go home. He was a rather good pool player. If they played any games at home, it might be horseshoes. He was good at that. More often, though, it would be cards. He would play gin rummy or if there were four of them, maybe euchre. Laverne was a formable opponent at cards. He had an excellent card sense, perhaps from his bridge game experience and seemed to know what was in his opponent's hands. It was tough to beat him, but the boys always wanted to try.

After David's freshman year in high school, the family moved to house in Irondequoit, a suburb on the northeast side of Rochester. The house was a little bigger. It had a detached two-car garage with a shed on a larger piece of property. They purchased this house. There was a lot of open land around the house. There was a good 10 acres or more directly behind the property as well as a big open field across the street. Plenty of space for a teenage boy to explore. Beyond the field across the street there were railroad tracks. Beyond that was a steep embankment that let down to the Genesee River. Wow, David could be Huck Finn! It was kind of like moving back to farm country in fact there were some farms up the street. It did not take too long before Denny got a job working for a farmer who produced and sold a horseradish sauce. At times, David worked for him too. The boys also earned some money, depending on the season raking leaves or shoveling snow. Occasionally, they mowed the lawn during the warm months. Laverne would never tell them to do that. He would be out pushing the old rotary hand mower and Lena would see it and tell one of them to go help their dad. They always had to be told to do it. Laverne liked the new property because he could plant a garden in the back. His favorite vegetable was yellow beans. When they ripened, he would pick a bunch and Lena would cook them with some potatoes and milk in a big pot. That was supper and it was good too, although they do not remember anyone else ever eating yellow beans that way.

The boys generally got good report cards usually all A's and B's. Laverne would look at the report and grunt and that would be that. Lena would hardly say anything. Most parents would be pleased and praise their children for good grades. Not so with the boys, it was expected. It was much later when they were adults, married and on their own that Lena expressed how proud she was with them. She told them then of how she was called into school for a conference one time, expecting to be told about something they had done wrong. When she arrived, a school representative told her how well they were all doing and what fine boys she had. She was proud and I think Laverne was too. It just did not always get communicated down to the boys though. They rarely brought their friends over to their house, they usually spent time at theirs.

The move had another benefit. God saw their need for praise and maybe someone to talk to that understood them a little better. Up the end of their street and just around the corner lived Lena's younger sister, Marion, her husband Bob and her three children Eileen, Suzy, and Karen. The boys now had relatives nearby and they spent a lot more time at their house. Eileen was older and about to leave the nest. Suzy and Karen were closer to Denny and Doug's age. The real benefit though was Aunt Marion. She had raised her own children. She knew better how the boys felt. She would talk to them and more important, she would listen. She became a buffer helping them see Laverne and Lena's point of view. She would also talk to her sister and calm things down when there was conflict. It became a tradition to have Thanksgiving dinner at Aunt Marion and Uncle Bob's house every year. That was a feast. Aunt Marion was good cook. The boys also were introduced to Uncle Chuck Siegel (Lena's younger brother) and his wife Rosemary and their two children Lynn and Wayne. Their kids were much younger than David, Dennis, and Douglas. Everyone would gather at the Siegel house at Christmas and found that Aunt Rosemary was a rather good cook also. They seemed to accept the new boys readily and that was a blessing.

Lena, Laverne, Bob, Marian   Denny, Karen, David, Doug, Suzy

David's first steady job came at age 16 working after school and weekends at a burger restaurant near the beach on Lake Ontario. It was called the Charbroil and was a hangout for just about everyone in the area. The Owner, Russ, ground his own hamburger meat, hand cut his steaks and made some of the best onion rings ever. The job included everything from washing dishes, sweeping floors, helping grind the meat and waiting on tables earning the huge sum of $1.05 an hour. The bicycle provided transportation to and from work and back and with the job came independence.

The independence meant David did not spend a lot of time at home, especially on weekends. One summer day he decided to go check on his anchor again and rode his bicycle back out to the farm. He was not running away this time just visiting. Mrs. Harris was sick at the time but seemed happy to see him. She bombarded him as they sat in the living room with questions about David and his brothers. "Does Doug still do…? Does Denny still have the habit of.. Are you still playing the cello? Etc." He does not remember all that she asked but every question was a question a mother would ask. He knew it. He felt it. She was still his mom. The anchor was secure. When David was about to leave, Grandpa Harris handed him two silver dollars and told him that he and mom Harris had taken in over 30 foster children over the years. Some had only been with them a few months; others like Marty all their lives to that point. He seemed genuinely appreciative that David had come for a visit. About 3 months later David learned why she was sick. he found out she had died of cancer. It hit him like a sledgehammer, and he was not in the best of moods when he went to the restaurant. Russ's niece, who also worked at the restaurant, got in David's face that night and he lost it. He slapped her and then realized he had better get out of there before he did something even worse in his anger. A little way away from the restaurant, he ran into her boyfriend. By then David was calmer. He told her boyfriend what had happened and that if he wanted to punch David out, he had the right. The boyfriend let it go. He knew what she was like. David was thankful but was also dejected. His anchor was giving way. Mom number two was gone. He knew that he could not rely on anyone but himself.

Things became a bit more difficult. David wanted to do things his way and resented some of Lena's, opinions. He had his own ideas on what he wanted to be and the colleges he might want to attend. When she voiced her opinions at times, David's temper led to some very verbal heated confrontations. She would tell his father. Laverne was generally calm but if he heard her complaints too often, he would come down on David with a vengeance. He would hit him with his open hand around the head and shoulders and all David could do was raise his arms up and take it. Laverne never really hurt his son, he just had enough of this mouthy teenager's backtalk and let him have it. Afterwards, he always felt remorse in losing his temper. David would sit in the den out of sight for a while to let things calm down. Lena also felt bad and talked to Laverne to check on his boy. He would come in and put his hand on David's shoulder. He would check David out to see if he were OK but did not say much. That would be that.

Senior year was eventful. David liked girls, but he was very shy. He attended the senior prom because a nice girl asked him not the other way around. It was an enjoyable experience, but the relationship did not go any further. David applied to several colleges and was accepted at all of them. He wanted to go to the University of Rochester, his mother's alma mater. Tuition was going to be too high, however. He did earn a regent's college scholarship due to his

SAT scores which would pay all four-year's tuition at a state school. He was excited to receive the scholarship. Lena's only comment was "So?" Laverne did not say anything. With the scholarship in mind, he elected to attend the State University College at Brockport, New York. Also, all young men his age just knew that as soon as they turned 18, they would be drafted. The Vietnam war was in full swing. He decided to get ahead of the game and joined the Naval Reserve and there was a contingent in Rochester. David was 17. The obligation included weekly meetings and two weeks every year. They deferred the active-duty commitment to anyone attending college. There was a small monthly paycheck and every bit helped while in school. He was preparing to leave home.

Denny initially got a job at Kodak. Denny got his driver's license before David did, and bought a car before David did. Of course, there was NO competition about that. Later he joined the Air Force. When he did, David bought the car from his brother (a 1960 Chevy) but did not pay him right away to punish him for buying a car before him. Of course, there was NO competition between them.

After High School, the boys each took separate paths, and their stories will be dealt with in the following chapters.

David   Dennis   Douglas

CHAPTER 14:
DAVID

D avid went to college at Brockport, New York about 20 miles from Rochester. He worked at his college studies majoring in physics and math. He also worked to help pay the bills. He kept up with his Naval Reserve obligation and even advanced in rank. Each year he had to go for two weeks. The first time was boot camp in Chicago. The second was aboard the Hartley a destroyer escort (DE 1029) out of Newport, Rhode Island.

The Hartley

That was the first time he had ever even seen the ocean and he went to sea cruising down to Virginia Beach. The weather was terrible squall conditions, and the ship was constantly pitching and rolling in the monstrous waves. He was seasick a good part of the time but still had to take his turn standing watch on the bridge a position about 20 feet above the waterline at the dock. He was dry heaving continuously during his evening watch. Later, he went below to his bunk and went to sleep. He was jolted awake with a collision alarm at about 4 AM. Someone hollered at him to get up, get dressed quickly and get up on deck. A Norwegian merchantman (Blue Master) had collided with the ship off Virginia Beach. When he got up on deck, someone ordered him to get on a life jacket. David made his way quickly aft down the port side of the ship and then up the starboard side where he faced twisted metal and water over his ankles. He looked out from the ship and there was a huge wave coming right at him. He froze for a second then turned around and quickly retraced his route. Someone threw him a life jacket. He looked out the port side of the ship and spotted land. That made him feel better until he looked more closely in the dim light and saw huge waves crashing down on the beach. Meanwhile the ship started to list to the starboard. His sea sickness was cured.

God was with the David even then. The lookouts had spotted the Blue Master long before it hit the ship and reported it to the officer in charge. He was inexperienced, however, and did not realize the danger. The captain was not on the bridge initially but came up just five minutes before the collision. He assessed the situation and tried turning away. When he realized there was not enough time, he ordered a full ahead and a hard-right turn toward the tanker. That action saved all lives on board.

The Blue Master's bow tore into the Hartley on the starboard side about two-thirds of the way aft. The stern of the ship was moving away to minimize the blow. The bow of Blue Master stopped just 3 feet from the ship's keel. If it had cut the keel, the two halves of the ship could have sunk right there, and that may have been the end of David's story. There were other stories as well. The bow of the tanker came into one officer's stateroom and the officer used that bow to climb out to safety. Another man had just gotten out of the shower when that tanker bow crushed his shower stall. Another had just gotten a drink out of a vending machine when the machine was hit. The bow destroyed sickbay but there was no one in there at the time. Amazingly there were no lives lost and no one was badly hurt, only the ship. The collision cut all power and ship control. Several men including David were ordered to the bow of the ship to manually drop the anchor to keep the ship from washing onto the beach. While there, a huge wave crashed over the bow and drenched David from behind. Then he did a stupid thing, he turned around. The next waved finished the job. Sunrise brought some tugboats, and they shot a line to the ship so that the crew could pull a big rope hawser through the bullnose on the bow and down the port side of the ship. They pulled it all the way aft, but no one thought to secure it. When the wind picked up and the tug started to pull away, 60 guys, David included, let go of the hawser. At the end of it was a loop that streaked by missing all of them by mere inches. If any one of them had been caught in the loop, it could have torn them apart especially as it screamed through the bullnose. The next attempt was more successful. The anchor was pulled, and they were towed into dry dock. Once inside, the water was pumped out and the entire ship then sat on supports so that the engineers could assess the damage. David walked to the apex where the Blue Master's bow had stopped and looked down. He could see straight down through the ship to the engineers below looking up at him. God was there that day. There were other cruises but none as exciting as the first!

David had a full schedule, but there was time for dating. He dated one girl exclusively for a couple of years. Then there was a period where he dated three beautiful girls, Debbie, Cheryl, and Jan at the same time. That did not last long. He finally dated them one at a time, but it was Jan that really turned his head. She was the daughter of Milton and Florence Hilfiker. They were dairy farmers living in Holley, New York. She had an older brother Jerry, a younger brother Ed and two younger sisters, Christine, and Kathy. David loved going to that farm. In one sense, the anchor he had on the Harris farm was being restored in the Hilfiker family.

Milton and Florence Hilfiker and the old farmhouse

Chris, Jerry, Florence, Jan, Milton, David, Ed, Kathy

During that time, Jan was finishing her nursing studies, working, and living with a lifelong friend named Dottie. Denny came home on leave from the Air Force. Jan and David introduced him to Dottie. That was it. A few short months later they were married.

Later David asked Jan to marry him and eventually she said yes. They were married June 20th, 1970. Jan became his pride, his companion, his friend, and his lover ever since. Laverne was quiet with the first girl David brought around, warmed up some with Debbie and Cheryl but was all smiles when it came to Jan. Watching his father's reaction, David knew he had chosen the right one.

Graduation came in 1968 and he was awarded a Bachelor of Science degree in physics. Laverne and Lena attended graduation and for the first time in his life, Laverne held out his hand to shake his son's hand. That simple gesture spoke volumes. Laverne was proud of his son. He went active duty as a rated Sonar man with a four-year degree. The Navy decided to send him to instructor school and then down to fleet sonar school in Key West Florida. He ended up working for a coast guard chief who managed a basic electricity and electronics programmed instruction course. The chief was an administrator and did not know much about the subject, so it became David's course. He loved the duty and fell in love with the Florida Keys. His major worry during that time was whether he could go fishing with the chief and his friend on his friend's boat on Wednesday afternoons.

Jan and David's Wedding

Jan's father Milton and her mother Florence   David's father Laverne and Lena

Jan and David drove down to Key West to start their life together. On the way in south Miami, they picked up their "honeymoon" baby, a dachshund puppy. They named her Jennifer Renee. They were kidded later about her name; some of their friends told them that they named their dog better than they named their kids. Jan and David rented a one-bedroom apartment. It was cheap. It did not have air conditioning (Jan took three showers every day to cool off). They put together two single beds to make one bed. That bed was a backache in the making. One quarter was high, one quarter was low, and the rest was somewhere in between.

David and two friends, Geoff, and Jerry started a singing group to perform at the "Ye Old English Pub" on Big Coppitt key about 10 miles north of Key West. Jerry played a good blue grass style guitar along with an autoharp, David played some guitar.

Geoff did not play an instrument, so they made him one, a "gut bucket". A gut bucket is a wash tub base made from a wash tub, eye bolt, broom handle and a piece of twine. The broom handle stretches the twine, which when plucked produces a base sound. It was a mix of country, blue grass, folk, skits, and whatever else came into their heads done without any amplifiers or microphones. The pub served beer and wine and sold a cheese plate. The main beer on tap was Watney's Red Barrel from England and so they named the group "The Red Barrels". No one made much money, but they had a lot of fun. The main shows were done on Friday and Saturday evening and soon they had a good group of regular patrons. Half the time they did not even know what they were going to do until they got up and did it. The owners created skits for them to perform as part of the show. They spoofed everything. In one skit, they enlisted a girl to lay on a stretcher with some dolls on her stomach and a blanket over the dolls. She was supposedly being interviewed by a hospital administrator, Geoff, for admission into the hospital. Meanwhile, she began giving "birth" pulling out a doll one at a time, spanking it and laying aside. Geoff totally ignored her until he determined that she had a piggy bank and that there was enough money in it to admit her. The skit ended with the girl being carried out and Geoff asking her: "Now what seems to be the matter?" In another skit they told the audience that Professor Van something was going to play Bach for them. Geoff then came out like a classic concert pianist complete with tux and tails and sat down very prim and proper on a bench. There was no piano. After he very stiffly sat down, he pulled out a kazoo from his pocket and proceeded to play Bach with all the seriousness of an actual pianist. The audience nearly fell off their seats they were laughing so hard.

Jerry, David, Geoff

The pub was fun and family. Regulars came to relax, have a good time, and spend some time with friends. The trio was paid a percentage of the total sales and there were also tips. A dollar was a good tip. One man had an unusual way of tipping them. He would put a dollar in something, a cigarette, a bar of soap, a dollar inside a light bulb, etc. The entertainers were also entertained.

The Navy decided to release David early. He wanted to stay on the Keys, so he applied and was hired by the Monroe County School district to teach school at Coral Shores in the upper Keys. Jan went along with it thinking that David would get this Keys thing out of his system and then they would go back home to Rochester.

She also got a job as a nurse at a small hospital near the school. They still made the trek down to the pub every weekend for a while; they just limited to Saturday nights. After the pub, they would drive 80 miles home in a Fiat roadster. David loved seeing how fast he could go on the old 7-mile bridge late at night. God had to watch out for them then. That bridge was so narrow that the buses routinely knocked their mirrors off as they passed each other. David loved it; Jan was quietly terrified.

After a while Jan was pregnant. David had prayed for a girl first and God answered. He gave them Amy Lynne. She was a beautiful baby from a beautiful mother and David was enthralled.

At a couple of month's old David wrote a song for her. He added the second verse after she started walking at 8 months. The song went like this:

Amy's Song

I've got a baby the cutest little baby
The prettiest little baby and I don't mean maybe.
She's the apple of my eye and she's even got the prettiest little cry.
She wears her diaper at a rakish angle
prettiest little foot and cutest little ankle
As she lays there her hands all curled

prettiest little baby in the whole wide world,
prettiest little baby in the world

And I can see I'm going to have a tough time
Keeping those little boy babies in line
And I don't know as I want the world to see
'fraid somebody's going to take her from me

And as she comes up to me all smiling
Two bottom teeth and the top ones a tryin'
She does a little dancing to my guitar
There's not another baby that's prettier by far

Later David was hired by the Coral Grill in Islamorada. They set him up with a couple of microphones, one for his voice and the other for the guitar. It was fun. The owners and patrons seemed pleased. One of the best compliments he got was from the owner who said that they were having some trouble getting people out of the bar to go to their table. Wow! Later, one of his students, Bill, joined him. He played the guitar better than David and had a good voice. Bill learned enough of David's routine that one time he reached around David and chorded the guitar as David strummed it. The audience seemed to enjoy the antics. David's brother Denny had his own view of the entertainment as illustrated in his cartoon.

John David was born three years later and that was a trip. When Amy was born, David and Jan drove over an hour to get the hospital in South Miami and Jan was only in labor about a total of four hours. Second babies often come quicker, and they had a lot further to drive this time. David was nervous. Jan casually woke him early in the morning and made him breakfast. When they got on the road, David was a wreck thinking they were not going to make it. When they got there, he parked in the wrong place and they had to walk through a good part of the hospital. The doctor checked Jan, quickly pushed David out of the way, and wheeled her into the delivery room. Fifteen minutes later, they came out and told David that he was now a father to a healthy baby boy.

Four years later, Jan became pregnant again. This time at the first sign of any labor pains, David was pushing her to the car and prepared to break every speed limit to get them there. She calmed him down. They got to the hospital without incident. This time though, that baby had other ideas. After twenty-four hours with no increased labor, the doctor sent them home. Two weeks later they made the trip again. Again, another long labor. Their daughter, Lisa Anne, had other ideas about coming out from her nice warm womb. Every time Jan pushed; she would move to the side rather than down. Finally, the doctor decided to induce labor. Then everything happened very quickly. David did not watch the birth of Amy and John, but the rules changed this time, and he could watch. Every father ought to watch. When she came out, even covered with whatever babies are covered with, he thought she was the most beautiful thing he had ever seen in his life. She was crying as they put her in her little bed. David talked to her and she stopped crying and listened. He said something stupid like "Now we have to get some rules straight around here". The doctor laughed.

David, Jan, Amy, Lisa, John   *David*

David's first-year teaching was a navy like seal boot camp for teachers. He taught six classes of 210 kids and had a homeroom of all 7th and 8th graders. The classrooms were only built for a maximum of about 24 students and with 30 plus in each class, the rooms were crowded. He spent most of my time in the classroom just trying to keep order and prevent kids from hurting themselves or other students. One student in one of the 8th-grade classes, for example, purposely smashed an alcohol burner on the floor and promptly set fire to the floor. There was also another problem called puberty. It was not too bad in 7th-grade, but it was very apparent in 8th-grade especially among the girls. David looked good to those young girls and they were always crowding around his desk to talk to him. Some of the more outgoing 8th graders even asked some more provocative questions. He had to tread very carefully. With all that going on, David developed migraine headaches, sometimes two or three a week.

There was some fun stuff as well. One very calm warm day a whirlwind appeared right outside the classroom door. David brought all the kids outside and they literally stepped into and out of it. It was not strong enough to do anything but blow hair around or lift a paper cup, but it sure provided a neat science lesson. In another instance his class of very noisy 7th graders were sitting along long tables in the room. They ignored his repeated urgings to be quiet, so he picked up a yardstick and slapped it down hard on one of the tables. There was a loud whip-like crack. The room became instantly quiet, and the students came out of their chairs and then back down again in unison. It was so funny to watch, that David had to turn around to compose himself; he was laughing so hard. Those kids could also be very quick witted. David wondered how one of his 7th grade girls named Ralphine got her name. He asked her if she was named after her father. Without missing a beat, she responded: "Yes, his name is "feen." She nailed him. The last week of that school year an 8th grader named Shirley handed him a coffee can full of cookies. She thanked him and told him that she would miss him next year. David got his bonus for the year.

The following year, a couple of teachers were leaving and there was an opening to teach high school chemistry, physics, and math. It required though, that David take another chemistry course, so he could become certified in chemistry. He was already certified in physics and math. He opted to take the class at his alma mater in Brockport, New York. That was not a problem for him, but it was a real strain on his wife. She had left her family and friends to follow David down to the Keys and she was awfully close with all of them. She had hoped that he would soon get this Keys thing out of his system and then they would go back home. Now he added insult to injury by going back for a month and a half to attend his old college. He even stayed with her parents. She had to stay back alone and work at the hospital. Some of the local police and others saw their chance and started hitting on her. If she were not such a moral person and committed to making the marriage work, it could have led to some real problems. She told David about the advances. When he got back, she introduced him to one of the most persistent suitors at a school function. David shook his hand, looked him in the eye, and said: "Oh you're the one that has been trying to make time with my wife". Jan was horrified and embarrassed. The man fumbled for something to say but after that, he stopped his advances.

David's reprieve from the rigors of teaching came as he explored the waters around the Keys. He bought a boat. As soon as he got it, he had to go out in it. He and a couple of other teachers went out after school during the week to go snorkeling out on the reef. When they decided to come back in, he learned he had made a big mistake. He had left the engine key turned on and ran the battery down. They could not start the engine. The sun went down, and it got dark, so they anchored up and huddled down inside the boat to keep warm. Meanwhile a frantic Jan called the Coast Guard to search for her missing husband. David and the others spotted the search boat in the middle of the night and nearly set the boat on fire trying to signal them. The Coast Guard saw the fire, came to them, and towed them back in. The Coast Guard could have cited David for not having the right equipment on board but decided not to. After that incident, David made sure he had all the equipment as well as a pull cord that he could use to start the motor in an emergency. God was with them that night and David learned his lesson.

Weather permitting, David was out in it that boat three or four times a week and Jan became a "boat widow". During the cooler weather, he would be out in the boat or on a channel bridge at night catching shrimp. There were quite a few nights when he and his friends caught a cooler full of shrimp many of those were jumbos. David's poor wife often ended up heading those tasty crustaceans and packing them for the freezer. If the weather was bad for a length of time, he was cranky and plain hard to live with. More than once he lost his temper because he could not get out in his boat. Occasionally Denny and Dottie would come down for a visit. Denny's view of the fishing was a little different than David.

The biggest fish they ever tackled occurred one summer when Jan came out with David. That day they went out with friends in two boats and fished at the Islamorada Hump about twelve miles out. The hump was an area in the gulf stream where the bottom rose sharply from about 450 feet to about 280 feet. There were always big fish hanging around. They fished for amber jack by dropping baits upstream of the hump. Then the fun began as they fought a thirty or more-pound fish up to the surface. David had one almost to the boat and Jan was trying to help him pull the fish in when a tiger shark came up and took a chunk out of the fish. It came within inches of Jan's hand. She nearly had a heart attack. David hollered to the other boat about the shark and they quickly threw out a baited hook. The shark took the bait. Eventually David climbed into their boat and one of the others took Jan back to the dock in David's boat. The shark fight continued for more than three hours and they dragged it back and hung it up at Holiday Isla docks. The shark weighed 560 pounds and measured nine-and-a-half-foot long. A local fishing paper snapped their picture, and they made the front cover that weekend. They disposed of the carcass, but David kept the jaw. Somehow Jan never wanted to fish with David after that.

Periodically, Laverne and Lena would come down for a visit and David would take his father fishing. There was a good chance that he would get seasick, but Laverne always wanted to go. He wanted to spend time with his son. Fishing was good and they had a few exciting days and brought back fish to eat. One time while fishing a patch reef, David landed an 85-pound jewfish (goliath grouper). Laverne thought that was the biggest bass he had ever seen and could not wait to show it to Lena.

Teaching high school proved to be a lot better. Those kids were all the better students with a real desire to do well. Those courses, though, were hard for them. It was a challenge to make it interesting and understandable. David did the best he could.

Sometimes he got into some trouble with the principle with some of the experiments. It seems they had not designed the ventilation system in the building correctly and vented a lot of the fumes from the chemistry classroom directly into the principal's office. David gassed him out more than once.

The last month of the school year, his predecessor had set up a qualitative analysis program for the students. It involved giving each student a liquid with some ions dissolved in solution. The objective was to go through a series of tests to determine what ions were present. There were also some solutions with known ions, so they could determine what would constitute a positive test. There were flame tests, color tests and precipitate tests. It took a while for the students to perform all the tests, but it really did give them a sense of being in a real chemistry lab.

Physics was also a challenge. David tried to use what he could to illustrate the physics principles, but it was still hard for the students. He was known as a tough but fair teacher.

Geometry was not every student's favorite subject. If you have never taken geometry, that is the time that students are given a set of mathematical facts and then, systematically, they are to reason using those facts to prove another conclusion is true. It is an exercise in logical thinking. The proofs lasted several weeks. When the students would come into class, David would pick one student as a judge and set them at the desk in the front of the classroom. He would pick another and make them the prosecuting attorney. The rest of the class was the jury. Who was on trial? David! To convict him the prosecuting attorney had to correctly complete the proof. If David could find 3 objections to whatever they did, he won the case. He told the jury that they could not help the prosecuting attorney. He told the class they were going to do this for a couple of weeks and then there would be a test. If they won more of the cases than he did, then he would forgo the test. Now the class was motivated. Every student was focused on the prosecutor. David did not have to look at the work on the board to know if the prosecuting attorney made a mistake. The class reactions told him. He would always wait a little before objecting. The class hoped he would not see the mistake. Eventually he would object and score one for the teacher. If he got up to three, there was a noticeable groan from the class. David had way too much fun with those sessions.

There were mistakes, times when he was angry, when experiments did not go exactly as planned, when students were upset either with him the school or life in general, etc. There were times he failed to communicate as well as he should have. As this section was being written, Jan pointed out that you could always tell when someone was self-centered; they always must be the center of attention. Add a corollary that; if they write something, look how much of it is in the first person using I, me, my, etc. David was guilty. God had a solution for that attitude, though, He started a spiritual war within David against the flesh desires.

It began when David was confronted about his spiritual condition. Jan was raised Catholic. David was not. David wanted Jan so he went through the indoctrination so that they could be married in her church. After that, Jan continued attending a Catholic church on the Keys, but David did not go with her. He told her that if they could find a church that they agreed upon, he would go to church with her. That continued for a while and then some friends invited them to their church. It was a small church meeting in what was originally a movie theater in Islamorada, Florida. They decided to try it out. That Pastor was preaching from the Bible and David had a lot of respect for that Book from the seeds planted in the Harris foster home. They began attending regularly but David felt every sermon seemed to be directed at him. He felt as though the Pastor was checking with Jan every week to see what he should preach on the following week. The Gospel message:

that all of us were sinners deserving of death and separation from God in hell,

that Jesus came to pay the penalty for our sins by dying on a cross,

that after three days He rose again and went back to heaven to prepare a place for them,

and that anyone including David could receive the gift of heaven by simply putting his trust in Him.

David heard the message week after week but did not respond. Many thought he never would. Deep down he was not sure he could trust God. After all He took mom and did not answer Laverne's prayers on her behalf. He could also sense that Laverne was angry at God. Although he did not realize at the time, he was also worshiping another God, science. He just knew that science could explain everything even how we got here. He had a tremendous respect for all those PhD scientists that had studied all aspects of existence. Whatever they said had to be true. If they wrote down that we evolved from simple life forms that spontaneously came into existence, then that is what he believed.

Certainly, these dedicated men and women would not write anything that was not true or purposely try to deceive people. The Bible clearly said, though, that:

"In the beginning God created the heavens and the earth" (Gen 1:1).

And that He did it in 6 days. David was conflicted. It really came to a head when one summer he taught a summer school biology class to earn some extra money. The textbook clearly taught evolution. A short time into the course, a young man in the class came up to him and said:

"Mr. McIntyre, why should I have to learn this? I do not believe in it."

David's reaction was not good. He became angry. Who was this student to tell him what to teach? Just as the exchange began to become more heated, David's supervisor who was a Christian happened to come by the class. She calmed things down. The class continued without further incident and the young man passed the course. David made a mental note that he was going to study and learn all the evidence proving evolution was true. The next student that challenged him was then going to be peppered with the evidence. God had other plans.

Around that time David and Jan decided to attend a movie night at the church. The movie that night was called: "A Thief in the Night". It was based on the passage in I Thessalonians chapter 5 depicting the "Rapture" of the church during the end times and then the tribulation period that would follow. The movie depicted this awful time in very graphic terms. It scared David. He just knew that he would be one of the ones left behind to endure the wrath of God. As the movie was finishing, he bowed his head and prayed earnestly for God to save him. He told God that he knew that he was a sinner deserving of death, and His wrath in hell. He understood that Jesus purchased a pardon for him on the cross. He told God he wanted to put his trust in Jesus to save him. Even as David ended the prayer, he was still fighting God. he looked around and thought to himself, no one saw me do that, did they? God did not let him get away with that. He heard a distinct voice in his head saying that he needed to tell someone. He did. Then, he felt the urging to get baptized. Jan and David did it together in the ocean at one of the church member's property. Later, he felt God saying that He wanted David to talk to Him in prayer. David remembers getting down on his knees beside the bed at their house. The door was closed, and he began to pray. Part way into the prayer, Jan opened the door and immediately David jumped up. God did not like that, so that same scene was replayed a few days later. This time he felt a hand on his shoulder and a distinct voice in his head saying: "This time, David, stay down and pray." Jan opened the door. David came up with all kinds of reasons why he should get up; He was going to lose respect, Jan is not going to like this, etc. but he stayed down. After a few seconds, which seemed like years had gone by, Jan did something he never expected. She went over to the other side of the bed and kneeled and prayed silently with him. That may have been the moment when Jan transferred the spiritual leadership in their family over to David.

God had taught David to talk to Him, so David asked Him to help him out with science and the Bible. God did. David was bombarded with book after book after book all written by scientists with earned PhD's from prestigious universities that did not believe in evolution. They made an incredibly strong case against evolution and for Biblical creation. They did so from the science that he knew and respected. He became convinced. Now he tells everyone that he has evolved. By an evolutionary process, he had become a creationist. Time passed, and David felt that others needed to hear some of the things that he learned. Under the direction of the pastor, he put together a 13-week Sunday school study series on Science and Scripture. He has repeated that class or parts of it many times over the years.

About 2 years later after the incident with the student in the biology class David ran into that young man again. David shook his hand and thanked him for standing up and challenging him. David told him that his challenge was instrumental in putting David on the right path.

When David accepted Christ, a war started. It was a war between David's old flesh, its ideas, needs, and wants and what God had in mind for him. The flesh fought God at every turn; coming to salvation, telling someone that he had received Christ, baptism, prayer, science versus Scripture. That war is ongoing 40 plus years later. The flesh tries to win some of those skirmishes. Thank God, though, the final battle has already been won. Heaven is David's home. While he is still here, though, God is constantly having to work on David.

David was also convicted that he should be sharing the Gospel message with others, especially his own family. One by one each of the children accepted Christ and were eventually baptized. The hardest nut to crack, though, was his father. Laverne was angry at God for not healing his wife, Rae. David witnessed to his dad for over twenty-five years as did his brother, Denny. It was interesting that it was Lena that would often initiate the conversation. She was raised in a strict Jewish home and anything "Christian" was frowned on especially by her mother. She liked the yearly tradition of the Christmas tree, however, and she secretly liked to listen to Billy Graham preach. She would tell David that at the end of his message, she really wanted to pray with him to receive Christ but somehow her mother's admonishments would ring in her mind. She liked to hear the story again and again though and would nudge David often from the back seat of the car with Laverne driving to tell it one more time. David remembers telling her for the last time while she was in a coma shortly before her death. Perhaps she heard and maybe gave in and accepted Christ. David has a hope that she did. His dad resisted until about three months before his death. He finally gave in and prayed with Dennis to receive Christ. Dennis relates the story as one of the biggest blessings in his life in the next chapter.

God's biggest battles were with David's anger and pride. David did not see that he had a problem. Everyone is overly sensitive to the shortcomings in others but can be totally blind to their own. Even if people acknowledge they have a problem, they often minimize it or convince themselves that it is not as bad as it really is. All three boys have the anger problem. It may well stem from losing Rae at such a young age. David can look back now and see how God brought people in his life to teach him or mirror his problems back to him.

More often than physical confrontation, the anger manifested itself in physical destruction or a putdown of others. He would break things or make others feel inferior, stupid, or insignificant. He knew he was angry when he broke things. He was often totally insensitive, though, to the rest of it. Complicating the issue was his pride. He really did feel he was better than others in some respects and so he came across as condescending, and arrogant. He did not realize it; he just thought that he was being patient and helping others understand things better. He was oblivious to their feelings.

If he had one of his "I going to break something moods", everyone got out of the way. Wrenches would go flying if he were working on something. In one instance, one of the cars had broken down near the house and needed to be pushed home. David's brother Doug had come down and was trying to help by steering the 1965 Barracuda that had the problem. When he did not do exactly what David wanted him to do, David smashed the brand-new Fiat roadster into the back of the Barracuda denting both bumpers. Anger got the best of him again. Jan never quite knew when he would explode next. She was in fear of him. Later, after they had kids, the anger would come out against them. More than once she got between David and the children ready to take the blows if they came. Her gutsy confrontations stopped him. He loved his wife and never wanted to hurt her. She should not have had to put up with that kind of anger, however. There was some warning in the form of a glaring look or a sharp word. She once told David that he was acting like a little kid with a temper tantrum. He never thought of it as an adult temper tantrum, but she was right. He was acting like a self-centered child.

The more insidious version of his problem came in the form of putdowns. He knew when he was angry. Much of the time, though, he did not realize that he was belittling someone else. In fact, he often thought he was helping; even taking extra time to help the other person better understand the situation. He was totally oblivious to how his words, actions, and demeanor were being received by the other person or persons. The following are examples.

David eventually left the high school teaching job for an instructor position with Coulter Electronics, a medical instrument company. Later he became a senior instructor with the responsibility of training new instructors. That is when the problem showed up. If they detracted from how he did it, he just took over and showed them again how it should be done. In his mind, he was just "helping them." He was oblivious to the fact that he belittled them. His supervisor finally took him out of the classroom for a month to alleviate the problem. David was shocked! God hit him with a "two- by-four" to get his attention. That was the longest month he ever spent working for the company. God had given him the gift of teaching. Others around him and his students seemed to confirm that gift. He made the mistake, though, of thinking that it came from him not from God. That is always a huge mistake. He was better for a while.

Some years later, another instructor with equally strong opinions to David's mirrored his attitude back to him. It led to some heated confrontations. That was a second two-by-four. It suddenly dawned on David that the way he was treating the other instructor was exactly the way this other instructor was treating him. He began to reflect on all the other past interactions with the other instructors and wondered how often he had done the same thing to them. Also, why had he not been sensitive to it. He made it a point also to go back to that other instructor and ask forgiveness for his bull-headed behavior. After that, David knew he could not trust his own perceptions because he had been totally oblivious to the problem. He asked God for help and a partner or two that would periodically reflect to him a true picture of his behavior. He had one in his precious wife. He sought others at work. He needed them too.

The worst putdowns did not occur at work; they happened at home. It is difficult, but David had to admit he had hurt his wife. Again, he did not realize what he was doing. In his mind, he was explaining things or taking the time to clear up misunderstanding. What he did not realize was that virtually every time he was "explaining" his voice tone would become sharper, he would become louder, and more emphatic. He was condescending, belittling, even questioning her intelligence all the while thinking he was "helping her" better understand the situation. He was oblivious to how his attitude and actions were being perceived. People are blind to their own faults yet can easily see the faults of others even their own faults in others. He could not see it in himself. He did not understand why his wife would walk away and be angry with him; after all he was only explaining.

Anger is a McIntyre family problem. It is also one that must be constantly kept in check. A person with anger issues should think like the alcoholic that confesses that he is an alcoholic and only a one drink away from falling back into that sin. It is also good to have a partner to help. David is thankful for God's precious gift of his wife Jan who tells him when he is doing it again.

David and Jan now had three children under their care, and it became clear that Jan's full-time job needed to be the children. She gave up her nursing job. She did pick up some money babysitting, but David needed to be the major breadwinner. That meant some changes. David had to give up his boat. Next year he learned that Coulter was going to move the school out of the Keys up to Miami. That crushed David and Jan. They loved the Keys all their friends were there and did not like Miami. They got a little reprieve to get used to the idea because it would take Coulter about 2 years to find a location, buy or lease the property, and turn the building into a school. They began to pray about the move. If they were going to have to leave the Keys, they prayed that they would be able to sell their house on the Keys and buy a three-bedroom two bath house on an acre of land. They wanted a more country-like instead of a big city atmosphere to raise the kids. That was a huge prayer. Housing prices were double and more what they had paid for their house on the Keys. Interest rates were at 14 percent making it difficult to sell their house and buy another one. After a little bit of looking, they found a three-bedroom two bath house on an acre in unincorporated Broward County about 18 miles north of the new Coulter school. They liked the house and the country location but at first, the price was a bit out of their reach, and they had not sold the keys house. It was looking bleak. They prayed harder.

The Coulters valuing their instructors and realizing the difficulty, decided to help the situation. They sponsored a bridge loan for anyone trying to sell their house to use the equity in their present house as a down payment on a new house. They agreed to pay all interest accrued on the bridge loan for up to a year and a half to give the instructors time to sell and buy a new home. At the same time, the owners of the house in Broward lowered their price. David and Jan purchased the Broward house and moved into it in the fall of 1982. They rented the keys house while they were waiting for a buyer. They got another break at the last minute also; the bank reduced the interest on the new mortgage from 14 percent to 12. Financially, the move was hard on the family. It seemed that everything doubled. The mortgage payment was double what they had been used to. David would have to drive 18 miles one way to work instead of 3 miles on the Keys. They had obligated themselves to bring up the children in a Christian school and when they found what they felt was a good one, the tuition was much higher. There were a lot of months they wondered how they were going to pay the bills. On top of that, there were no buyers for the Key's house. A year went by. Another four and half months went by without a buyer and they were closing in on the end of the bridge loan when they would have to pay that interest as well. In desperation, they got a new realtor from their old church on the Keys. They found a buyer a few weeks later but the closing would have to be after the end of the bridge loan. The Coulters stepped in again and agreed to pay the additional bridge loan interest. David and Jan did not realize until later that they were the ones that benefited the most from the generous offer. A few months after everything was done, David and Jan found out that the bank holding the bridge loan failed. David and Jan knew that God had been orchestrating everything behind the scenes. David wondered, though, why God had waited so long to sell the keys home and put them under such duress. God brought him the answer. They were earning an extra one hundred and fifty dollars a month in rent on the keys house for a year and a half to help pay the bills. God is good and knows what He is doing even when we cannot see it.

There were other minor miracles. A couple of times money would show out of the blue right at the time they needed it. There was an anonymous gift of four hundred dollars one month. In another instance, several hundred dollars was rebated to them from an insurance company. How often does that happen. Somehow the bills got paid. When the vehicles needed to be replaced, somehow, they found something they could afford. God even seemed to help with repairs. In one instance, David was driving home in an old Toyota Corolla when the car developed a leak in the heater system inside the car. David pulled off the side of the road and prayed. The leak stopped. He then had a choice to make; drive to a garage and go into more debt to repair the leak or trust God and go home. He chose to drive home. As he was driving, he kept glancing down to see if the leak would start up again. It did not. As he was about to turn on his street, a thought occurred to him that it would be just like God to start the leak again when he was safely home. It did, just as David turned the car off in the driveway. He reached down and found a hose that literally disintegrated in his hand as he touched it. There was no way that hose would have held up to the pressure and not leaked without God holding onto it. David replaced the hose with a new piece for about a dollar. God wants to be part of our lives even in the little things.

There were some big things too. Twice the banks lowered their interest rates. David and Jan were able to consolidate their debt with a smaller payment. The last time, they got a loan for 15 years with a lower monthly payment and were able to completely pay off the house. That house grew from an initial investment of $85,000 to over a half a million dollars. Their country home, that people kidded that they had moved to east Naples in the beginning, became a premium place to live after many years in the township of Southwest Ranches. In another instance, after the Coulter brothers died the Coulter family decided to sell the business. It was sold to Beckman and the name was changed to Beckman Coulter. The Coulter family gave bonuses to all the Coulter employees in the amount of $1,000 for every year they had been employed by the company as a condition of the sale. David had been with the company 22 years by then and his share was $22,000 minus taxes.

God also had not forgotten David's love of the waters on the Keys. When he got down some friends, Kris, and Ginny, who owned a resort just north of Marathon on the keys would invite the family down, put them up in a two-bedroom rental place, let them enjoy their facilities, feed them, and take David fishing. What a blessing! David got regular raises and eventually they were in a better financial position. Kris and Ginny later moved out of the keys to South Carolina and David got wind that they had a Boston Whaler that they really could not use. He persuaded Jan to buy the boat and now he could go back and explore the waters off the Keys again. Laverne, Denny, and even David's son John was able to join them. Laverne especially enjoyed going to Flamingo to fish. The waters were calm there, like fishing in a creek, and there were plenty of fish, some fairly good size. Laverne liked to bet his sons a quarter on the first, the biggest, and the most fish. He had a good chance of winning the quarters and was all smiles when his sons had to pay up.

Laverne, David, and John at Flamingo, 1996

Many trips were made to Flamingo. David also found a fishing buddy, Wayne, in the church that he and Jan now attended. God really showed up in one such trip. It was a Monday on a holiday weekend. The fishing had been great, and they were heading home on Krome Avenue well north of Homestead when a tire blew on the boat trailer. At that time, the road was without any shoulder, and they were forced to just keep going. By the time they reached a gas station, the tire was shredded. David did not have a spare. It was winter about 5:00 PM and starting to get dark. Wayne was sure that it was going to be a long night because they were nowhere near any tire stores and now the rim was also damaged. God prompted David to pray with Wayne about the situation. After the prayer, they unhooked the boat, Wayne handed David what cash he had and the keys to his SUV, and David set out to search for a new rim and tire. He prayed as he drove. He drove in a large circle around the area and was almost back to Krome Avenue when he spotted an auto parts store. He stopped, went in, and found a tire display at the back. The exact tire and rim he needed was at the top of the display. David persuaded the store manager to sell it to him. He threw it in the SUV and drove back to Wayne and the boat. They quickly changed the tire and were back on the road. The whole process only took about an hour and a half. Both men learned something about God and power of prayer that day.

When finances got even better, David started trying to talk Jan into buying a new boat. Jan did not agree. David had learned by that time not to force his will on a big decision like that. God had taught him to wait. Sometime later Jan told him to go buy his boat. He researched, negotiated, and bought an 18 ½ foot Scout with a 115 horse Yamaha 4-stroke motor and trailer. It was the best and most reliable boat he ever owned. David's friend, Wayne, kept getting better and bigger boats. David began to spend so much time on Wayne's boat that he realized he did not need to have his own boat. He sold the Scout. God brought friends to David and Jan that have been continual blessings to them.

David and Jan's biggest blessings are their children and grandchildren. There were difficult times as they were raising Amy, John, and Lisa; times when they had to go to prayer a lot, but God protected them, kept them away from big problems. When a man tried to snatch Lisa in a Sears store, God made sure he failed. When Amy spun out of control across a multi-lane highway and crashed into a pole and totaled her car, God was there to protect her. She walked away with just a few scratches. Even though John had a great deal of difficulty in school, somehow God helped him do enough to pass and earn a high school diploma. When the kids started a fire in the house, somehow, they put it out and only the kitchen was damaged. Even in relatively small ones they learned their lessons. All three have good work ethics, try to do right, and most important, have accepted Christ as their Savior. Each one is trying to raise their own children well. All seek the council of mom and dad and that is a tremendous blessing. The grandchildren are close to their grandparents especially Jan. She had the privilege of taking care of each one early on in their lives. God created a strong family bond and nurtured it all their lives. It seems that God was always watching. When hurricanes came through, everyone was alright, and the house suffered only minor damage which insurance covered.

God is still in the blessing business. Recently when David wanted to sell his 10-year-old Pilot, he arranged for David to buy a much newer Acura MDX from their daughter, Lisa, who wanted to get out from under the high monthly car payment. The price was a whole lot lower than the $56,000 list price for a new MDX. In addition, Lisa's immediate family was about to expand and the house that she had just totally remodeled in Coral Springs, Florida was going to be too small for her. She offered to sell it to her parents. Jan loved the house and so they put the Southwest Ranches house up for sale. They had a buyer in four days and were able to buy the bigger newer house for a lot less money than they were selling their old house. Finances also allowed David and Jan to pay off the MDX and own it outright. It was a whirlwind transaction but when the dust settled David and Jan were in a new house with new appliances, a gorgeous view with extremely low upkeep and no yard work. Jan thought she was on vacation every day. They also live much closer to two of their children and grandchildren. There are blessings every day, we just must look for them.

CHAPTER 15:
DENNIS

The accounts recorded in this work are accurate. Dennis never remembers his mother, but knew she loved him. The super eight movies he viewed with Aunt Effie showed how much she enjoyed frolicking on the floor with all three of her sons. The love he felt quickly left him when she died. The foster homes began with bitter memories. His heart was filled with the thought, "Doesn't anyone love me?" The manikin on the shelf was so frightening to him, that he beat the bottom of the door and cried until passing out. To him, it was a mummy soon to come back to life. Between the ages of three and six, unhealthy demons would take their residence inside him. Three years of a loving mother's love, followed by three years of agony, had a tremendous effect on Dennis. He longed for the life he had during the first three years. The Harris farm offered great relief. He learned to jump into haylofts, ride cows and horses, pedal a twenty-six-inch bike, and eat cheerio ice cream bars when the barrel of treats arrived with Mr. Harris.

Still, his favorite memories during those formidable years were the times Laverne came to visit. He hoped that the next visit would be for good, and Laverne would take three boys to live with him. The Harris family had many positive effects, but Dennis never felt they were his parents. He remembers one day, when a rattlesnake was ready to strike a few feet away. Dennis stopped abruptly and watched the snake coil tightly. Somehow, he was able to run back to tell Mr. Harris, who came with a pitchfork to destroy it. After the snake's head was cut off, Dennis still thought it would be dangerous, as the rattle kept ringing long into the night. On another occasion Mr. Harris cut off the head of a snake and a small toad leaped out. The lump in the snake's neck must have been the toad's recent home. It was an amazing sight to see that the toad escaped, seemingly unharmed. Sunday dinners at the Harris farm were also a welcomed time yet being with his father meant everything.

When Laverne remarried and the family was united once again, things would be better, or so Denny thought. The first house on Brayton Road was unique in one way. The main living areas were painted red, even the ceilings. Dennis remembers watching Laverne paint many coats of white paint, only to see the red bleed though later. Eventually, it was covered. School came, relatively, easy. The high school years began after moving to the larger home in Irondequoit. Content with A's and B's, Dennis spent much of his after-school time working. Farmers nearby had plenty of work at

$.75 per hour. Green bean harvest was especially profitable as a farmer would pay $.35 per picked peck and Dennis picked five per hour. Mr. Roller had a horseradish business only a short walk from home. Saturdays were full of bottling operations at $1.25 per hour. Ron King was a boy, who lived a few houses up the hill. Dennis shared working with him and became best friends.

When not working for extra money, Dennis would work in the yard with Laverne. Sometimes, it was weeding the garden. On another occasion, it was helping to lay flat stones in cement for a patio. Laverne was always doing something around the house with enjoyment. His favorite non-work pastime was pitching horseshoes. He drove stakes at the forty-foot distance in the clay soil between sickle pear trees. Laverne won horseshoe competitions in the state and it showed each time his son played with him. Laverne would spot fifteen points with twenty-one being the winning score. Rarely, would Dennis win. On one occasion, Dennis threw five consecutive ringers, worth three points each. Then Laverne tossed six ringers on top. Laverne would place a single pear at the base of a stake and then throw a ringer without hitting it. It was amazing to watch. Although Dennis only remembers winning a game one time, the memories of playing with his dad were even better.

In addition to playing horseshoes, Dennis learned to play card games, especially, gin, bridge, and euchre. Laverne was always up to giving him lessons. This was one area that was shared until Laverne had a stroke toward the end of his life. Spending time with Laverne in that way was enjoyable for both. Laverne may not have showed his pride for his sons like other parents, but Dennis sensed it.

Like Rae, math and science were not difficult for David, Dennis, and Douglas. Each child used those gifts in their vocational paths, but in different ways. David became an instructor, where chemistry played a vital role. Douglas became a programmer. Dennis followed through with electrical engineering and technical training. David and Douglas used college as their initial path, but Dennis had no ambition for higher education after high school. He had a strong work ethic and desired to take a hands-on learning approach.

Knowing that the draft was in force, Dennis knew, that when he reached his eighteenth birthday, Uncle Sam would be at his door. He desired to continue to apply math and science as a career path, so he took the Air Force test to see what would be available. Test scores were high, and several options became available, especially in electrical engineering fields. Joining the Air Force became an easy decision. At that time, David was in college and fulfilling his military duty with the Navy. Laverne served in the army, and now two of his sons were following suit. That was a source of pride to him.

Although, attending church with the Harris family was mandatory, it was not a bad experience. Getting back with Laverne as a family was an answer to a child's prayer, but church became less important. After all, Laverne did not attend. Lena was Jewish. Meeting Dottie, changed Dennis' perspective on God, church, and more. The last thing he wanted to have was a girlfriend on his Christmas leave in 1967. Thanksgiving of that year was a disaster. The girl he thought was the one, was with another man when Dennis arrived at her house after a ten-hour drive. Driving back the same night was nearly disastrous as well. Joining David, his girlfriend, and her roommate for bowling sounded safe enough. Yet, one look at Dottie and Dennis was hooked. Before heading back to the base, he as much as proposed to her with a promise of marriage. Daily letters and high phone bills followed. After the wedding, one desire for both was to find a place to worship. Dottie was a Christian girl. Somehow, Dennis' lack of faith was not a deterrent for her.

Jan, Dottie, Dennis, David

Dennis became an autopilot specialist in the Air Force. It was a career path that shaped the rest of his life and God was opening doors of opportunity. The first door came, when Dennis desired to make the Air Force a career. Cancelled orders to Thailand, a new son, a guaranteed job at Eastman Kodak, and the thought of future separation from wife and family, made that decision less desirable. Still, the idea of going back to work in a non- electrical field weighed heavy. Kodak fulfilled their obligation by hiring Dennis, but as a handler. After a few months, a new apprenticeship opened within the company. Dennis applied for and was accepted into the electrical option. After three years, he would graduate as an electrician. This was a great step forward, but not engineering. Other areas were available for machinist, millwrights, and welders.

As an airman's wife, Dottie desired to work and earn extra income. She had experience in working for financial institutions and was able to secure a job off the base in Michigan. Dennis received orders to go to Thailand for the last year of his obligation. Dottie quit her job with the idea of moving back to Rochester, New York, near her family. God had other plans. The orders were cancelled. Without a job, Dottie discussed starting a family. Jeffrey David McIntyre was born on the Michigan Air Base on March 9, 1970. On August 8th Dennis completed his military obligation and went back to work at Eastman Kodak Company in Rochester. The idea of raising a family had an element of terror behind it for Dennis. He felt inadequate. A Free Methodist Church became a source of help, but his spirit remained restless. He provided by working many jobs, including cutting horseradish for Mr. Roller. He was able to get into an electrical apprenticeship at Kodak as well as a college night school program.

Dottie still desired to work and took a weekend evening position at a local hospital. She enjoyed it when Dennis watched their son. On the other hand, Dennis could not wait till she came home. As soon as the door to his home opened, his head hit the pillow with sound sleep. During the second child's pregnancy, Dennis became overwhelmed with fatherhood issues. He concluded that he needed help. One night he watched a Billy Graham crusade, and it was as if the message was directed directly to him. He knelt, confessed he was a sinner, asked God to forgive him and become Lord in his life. His daily prayer was to help him be a good father and protect his family should something happen to him.

Tricia and Jeff

When his daughter, Tricia, was under two years old, God left a message that was undeniable. He was in control. Dennis was picking up his grandmother across town on a Mother's Day when the phone rang there. It was Dottie. The message was short and disturbing, "Your daughter has been hit by a car, don't worry." The loud click on her hanging up nearly deafened Dennis. The thirty-minute ride across town was probably closer to twenty. Upon reaching home, calls were made to the doctor and hospital as no one was home. Finally, Dottie called from the doctor's office and he heard Tricia laughing in the background. Relief was an understatement. She was unharmed and a little dirty.

So, what happened? Neighbors had out of town guests who parked their car on the side next to Dennis and Dottie's driveway. The neighbor could see his quests as be started to back out of his garage but felt a light thump sound. He promptly stopped the car and looked up at his wife viewing from the kitchen window. She told him to not move and went out to the back of his car. Tricia had moved from behind the guest's car and was behind the rear wheel of the neighbor's car. Although covered with road tar, she was unhurt. When Dennis viewed the scene, it was obvious that this was a God miracle. Looking out of the kitchen window made it impossible to see a toddler behind and under the opposite car fender. Yet, she made exactly the right call. From that day forward Dennis did not need to pray for God's intervention over the lives of his family. He knew beyond a doubt that God was in control.

Laverne turned Sixty-five in June 1976 and decided to retire. His plans to take up golf, play pool with his buddies, and weekly bridge games could be realized. Dennis invited him to play golf one day with his brother, Doug. Laverne had only played a few rounds prior to that day with a makeshift set of old clubs. Doug had never played. They decided to give Doug a stroke per hole. If he took four shots on a hole, they would count it as three. The round began with the scores reflecting novice players. About the fourth hole, Doug stood on the tee and whiffed the ball on his first swing. Laverne let him swing again and not count the first one. Doug barely hit the top of the ball and it settled on the stone path in front of the green. That is one", Dennis yelled. Doug responded with, "That's zero" because you gave me a stroke per hole. Everyone chuckled. Then Doug hit the ball off the stone path, and it went into the hole. He yelled, "That's a hole in one." Again, everyone laughed as a whiff, a topper, and a stone putt counted as "1" on the scorecard. The very next hole provided even more joy. Doug already hit a shot and Laverne was ready to swing. For some reason, Doug stopped Laverne and asked why he was using a three iron on a 110-yard hole. Although he never played golf, he just hit a nine iron that far. A three-iron seemed like a club for a longer distance. Laverne shrugged it off, took his favorite club and slapped at the ball. It travelled about 100 yards, kicked onto the green and rolled up to the hole. Then he looked at his son and said, "That is why I used a three iron." Dennis was about to tee off and could not stop laughing. Then he looked up towards the green in time to see his father's ball fall into the cup. Without hesitation, Laverne said, "By the way, that's a hole in one." Dennis had played golf for many years without such a feat. It would be the only one this family would record. After Laverne's passing, the scorecard was proudly kept in his dresser drawer.

God had something to do with that day, though some might call it luck. Later that year, Lena and Laverne decided to move to Florida, where they could make their retirement income stretch. A rift was forming between them. Lena thought that Laverne would spend more time at home with her after retiring, but golf, pool, and bridge took up many hours away. A co-worker asked Dennis to bowl in a league every third week, replacing a trick worker, who would miss every third week. Dennis agreed. He bowled three games and then it was time to bowl again. The lanes were a drive across town. This time Dennis was concerned about Lena and Laverne's relationship following his retirement. He asked both to come for dinner. Then Laverne came to watch him bowl, while Dottie talked to Lena. The first game started out with a strike, and then Dennis would go off the lane to talk to his father. Another strike and Laverne would open a bit more. Understand that two or three words made a long sentence to Laverne. By the fifth frame, Laverne was talking more. That frame struck a strange chord in Dennis, as it looked more like a split than a strike. The 4-9 split stood after the ball went through the pocket and then both pins fell straight back in unison before the rack came down. Dennis returned to Laverne with a comment that seemed even stranger. The last time Laverne watched him bowl, another man had a 300 game. He told his father, "Gee, you haven't seen a 300 since the last time you saw me bowl." A perfect game is twelve strikes, and there were still seven to go. The words proved to be prophetic.

Perfect games were exceedingly rare in 1976. In this old establishment only one ever happened, previously. Nine other bowlers bowled on this pair of lanes with all games under 160. Bowling was halted to examine the lane conditions, pins, and the ball used as part of ABC (American Bowling Congress) rules. After about twenty minutes delay, all were approved, and the bowling resumed. During that delay, Laverne received council from his son about what to do to restore their relationship. Lena accepted Laverne's desire to play games and Laverne would be more open to her needs when he came home. They retired for several years to Florida with a much healthier relationship. God was at work with a hole in one and again with a perfect game.

Dad Sees 'Anxious' KPer Roll Perfect Game

After years of coming close, a bowler's dream finally came true for Dennis McIntyre, KP.

On Thursday, Oct. 14, Dennis bowled a 300 game at Empire Lanes. It was the second time he had ever bowled at Empire Lanes and it was his first perfect game.

Dennis credits his father with bringing him luck. When Dennis brought his father to watch the league bowl last year, someone else bowled a perfect game.

"I got a lucky strike in the fifth frame and told my father I was going to bowl 300," Dennis said. "After I bowled the ninth frame, I had a feeling I would go all the way."

Dennis said he got a little anxious toward the end of the game and almost bowled his 11th ball before the pins had been reset. When the last ball came up, Dennis said his only thought was to throw it like all the others.

"When I threw that last ball, everyone swarmed up on the alley," Dennis said. "I looked at my father and his face just lit up."

The perfect game was the first game of the night and Dennis followed it with games of 176 and 189. His average is 183.

Several times last year, Dennis missed perfect games by one strike. He also missed a chance earlier this year while bowling with his family at the EK Recreation Center.

On that occasion, Dennis had finished one game with five strikes and started the next game with a strike. As he approached the line for the second frame, his young daughter ran onto the alley and Dennis threw a gutter ball. He then finished the game with strikes.

Though he'll keep trying, Dennis does not expect to bowl another 300 game. "I think it's a once-in-a-lifetime thing," he said.

Perfect Game—Dennis McIntyre displays the form he used to bowl a 300 game.

The electrical apprenticeship was unique, however. The company desired to create a higher level of skills as technicians. One day a week would be dedicated to college classes. A Kodak worker, using the Rochester Institute of Technology curriculum, would teach these classes. At the end of the quarter, students would pay a small fee to go to the institution and challenge the course testing. One-third of a two-year degree would result at the end of the apprenticeship. Only Dennis and one other worker challenged and passed all the tests. No future apprenticeships were initiated like that afterwards. Yet, it opened the door for Dennis to complete a degree by attending school at night. College was not a real option for Dennis, but the company reimbursed all course costs.

The apprenticeship began to open more doors of opportunity. Programmed equipment was being introduced, which requires technical support. Dennis was assigned to the engineers designing the equipment and became their troubleshooter when the equipment was commissioned. This brought with it, financial increases as well as a desire to become an engineer. Another door opened in the engineering department as the need for more efficient and effective manufacturing equipment became necessary for the company to compete with competition. Electricians with technical skills could move into engineering as technicians, which had a higher pay level and room for advancement. Dennis interviewed for the position and was accepted.

The night school classes were immediately applied to the work Dennis performed. After about twenty years in engineering, Dennis retired as a full engineer, with five control patents added to his credit for the company, a feat that paralleled Rae's accomplishment.

United States Patent [19]

McIntyre

[11] Patent Number: 5,098,029

[45] Date of Patent: Mar. 24, 1992

[54] APPARATUS AND METHOD FOR MINIMIZING WEB CINCHING DURING UNWINDING OF ROLLS OF WEB MATERIALS OF INDETERMINATE LENGTH

[75] Inventor: Dennis A. McIntyre, Rochester, N.Y.

[73] Assignee: Eastman Kodak Company, Rochester, N.Y.

[21] Appl. No.: 531,983

[22] Filed: Jan. 1, 1990

[51] Int. Cl.⁵ B65H 23/08
[52] U.S. Cl. 242/75.44
[58] Field of Search 242/75.4, 75.43, 75.44, 242/75.5, 75.51, 75.53, 184

[56] References Cited

U.S. PATENT DOCUMENTS

Primary Examiner—Daniel P. Stodola
Assistant Examiner—John P. Darling
Attorney, Agent, or Firm—Charles E. Snee, III

[57] ABSTRACT

An apparatus and method for minimizing web cinching during unwinding of rolls of web material of indeterminate length. The position of the float frame or support member (36) of an accumulator (32) for the web is monitored and a proportional signal is sent to a comparator (52) which produces an increasing output signal as the float frame opens in the accumulator and a decreasing signal as the float frame closes. The output signal is fed to an integrator (66) which produces a gradually increasing or decreasing control signal for a voltage to pressure transducer (70) which operates a pneumatic brake (74).

8 Claims, 3 Drawing Sheets

His internal customers asked for him on future projects because the programs he wrote included diagnostics for those who maintained the equipment. This was part of who Dennis was. He knew that the equipment might be difficult for the electrician asked to debug it when it broke down. The built-in diagnostics helped to minimize the down time. Dennis loved to build new machines but did not desire to be on constant call for previous ones. It was a concept that would serve him long after retiring from Kodak.

After taking an early retirement, Dennis opened his own controls business and quickly was able to reduce the family debt load to a small mortgage payment. Although the business was doing well, God had other plans. Laverne had a stroke in his apartment in Florida. He was 87 and lived alone. After missing a second bridge date, a bridge partner contacted the apartment supervisor to check on him. He was alive, but unconscious by his bed. Three days without food and water and a cut on his head, might have been the end, but God sustained him. After weeks of treatment, Laverne was moved to a nursing home. At the time, he could barely swallow, lost the ability to read, and card playing was only a memory. After the stroke playing cards together was sad. Laverne knew he played but could not remember the rules. He also collected stamps and coins prior but lost the meaning. God took away all the things Laverne did to replace a relationship with his maker after losing his wife. Yet, through it all, God kept his brain receptive to receive Him before he passed.

Dennis resisted closing his business for several months, but God kept tugging at his heart. Part of his severance from Kodak was a year's salary, which he took as half pay for two years. The business reduced his debt load in Rochester, New York, to the point where this income would support his wife, Dottie, while he packed up the two-door accord and headed to Florida.

A friend had a business in Orlando, about forty-five minutes from Laverne's nursing home. He offered Dennis a position as a programmer for a new line of controls, which Dennis accepted. The salary was not great, but it would pay for an apartment. Saturdays and Sundays would be spent at the nursing home. Each trip involved securing a wheelchair in the small trunk of his car and lifting Laverne down into the front seat. Dennis could not bear seeing his father in that home any longer than he had to. Laverne also enjoyed the time away, although still bitter to God. David would come up occasionally and witness to Laverne as well, but his heart seemed to be hardened. On one occasion, Dennis had a thought about purchasing a used van to make the visitation process easier. By this time Laverne had been in the home for nearly two years and was approaching ninety. To make such an investment seemed unlikely, but not to God.

The following Monday, Dennis received a call at his workplace. "We would like to interview you for a position with Siemens." Dennis responded with the fact that he was unfamiliar with their product line. They assured him, that they would provide the necessary training. "You come highly recommended," was their reply. God was still working. It appears the engineering practices Dennis used at Kodak, somehow came to Siemens. They were looking for someone to represent them in the state of Florida to assist customers in applications. They asked what salary it would take to hire Dennis, who gave them his final salary as a Kodak engineer. They agreed. Then they said the position would include a vehicle, typically, a full-size car. Then, because of the size of the territory, suggested a van. Only a few hours earlier, Dennis entertained the idea of a van, and now it would be a reality. Not only would it be new, but also his two-door car could be used for Dottie when she made her visit.

Then another door was opened, the small one-bedroom apartment would become a nearly new house, which Dottie liked. The large increase in salary meant that such an investment would be better than rent payments. About three years later the house was sold for a sixty-percent profit, as home pricing soared in the state. God was still working out a detail that changed everything. On October 1, 2000, Dennis decided to be baptized by emersion at the church he was attending. He made the weekly trip to the nursing home. After fourteen months of witnessing, Dennis measured success, by getting Laverne to laugh. Little did he know that God had other plans that day. Upon lifting Laverne into the van's front seat, Dennis noticed the large print bible on the chair. It had been a gift from his son's, but Dennis knew he could not read it. After placing the wheelchair in the back of the van, Dennis began to drive to a favorite breakfast place. While on route, Dennis shared that this day would be cut short due to his scheduled baptism. After leaving the restaurant, Dennis placed the bible on Laverne's lap and asked if he was trying to read it. Laverne answered with the words; "I try. All I know is that I want to go to heaven where my three boys will be." Dennis could barely hold back the tears but asked if he knew how to get to heaven. Laverne responded with; "no," despite years of witnessing from his sons.

In the next few moments, Dennis told him "we are all sinners." Laverne quickly responded with; "I never did anything wrong." "Really," Dennis answered, and then asked him if he ever got angry or held a grudge." Laverne responded affirmatively. Then Dennis posed another question. "Suppose the creator of the universe looked down into this vehicle and saw you, would you think He would welcome you into his perfect heaven?" After responding negatively to holding a grudge, Laverne bowed his head and said, "no." Then

Dennis reassured his dad that God sent his only Son to die, so that none should perish. Laverne prayed three prayers. First, he admitted he was a sinner. Second, he asked for forgiveness. Finally, he asked Jesus to be Lord in his life.

After driving back that day, Dennis could not control his emotions. He called Dottie to share the news. Tears were running heavy, and Dottie could feel them. He called David as well. He was so caught up in the moment that he missed his turn and was almost late for his baptism. God had performed a miracle. Laverne was spared death in his apartment so that he would end his feud with God. God would take him a few months later.

Three weeks later, Dennis began to have doubts about his father's salvation. "How could a man eighty-nine years old with so many lost faculties, understand the commitment he made?" He asked for a sign. God would oblige. The following Saturday, Dennis went to visit Laverne and noticed that David had come the day before. He called his brother to see why he was not notified of the visit. David said that he had a day off and thought that Dennis would be busy with work. Then he spoke about something that happened on the visit. David took him to watch the pier fishing. On the way back, Laverne started singing. Dennis thought that was strange, as he had never heard his father sing before. Then David shared that it was not the fact that he was singing, but rather, what he was singing. Dennis wanted to learn more. David shared that he was singing, "When the Roll is Called Up Yonder, I'll be there." It was a hymn that came from Laverne's childhood. It was also the answer Dennis needed to confirm Laverne's salvation. About three months later David got a call from the nursing home about 7 AM on a Thursday morning just before he was to leave for work and told that his father had died in the night. David knew it was coming but it was still hard to hear. As he was about to turn onto the highway from his street, a song came on the radio that he had never heard before that began "If you could see me now…" God was there then too. It was just what David needed to hear.

"When the Roll is Called up Yonder" hymn was played at Laverne's funeral, where two people came forward. One was Laverne's apartment supervisor, who was Catholic. David's words in the eulogy touched the man to want to read the Bible. The second was the woman who played the songs. She said that she had been conducting services for twelve years and was never moved so much by a service. God was still working.

Later, Dennis wrote a book called, "Legacy of Love." He had some printed and spiral-bound for family members to read. God still had more to do. After Laverne's passing, Dennis questioned whether he should continue to work. Dottie was not ready for him to retire and desired that he not quit. The idea of working in Florida with a wife and home in New York weighed heavy. The God opened another door. It appears the process of learning the Siemens' programming had touched a nerve in the training center in Atlanta, Georgia. Dozens of documents on how to do Siemens' tasks made their way from Florida customers and salespeople. Dennis would write down each task and use the documents to help other customers. On one visit to Atlanta, Dennis was called into the training center and was asked to review a course manual. Dennis mentioned that it looked good, but the instructor said, "It should as it was your work." Dennis had opened a custom course offering, where customers could create a week of training to meet their specific needs. The training department wanted to hire Dennis at the first opening.

During that waiting period, Tricia Gallagher was about to have her first child. She was the daughter of Dennis and Dottie living in upstate New York. Dennis received an email from her, sharing that her husband, Adam, was looking to relocate to that area for a better job that would cover medical. Tricia was teaching and had medical benefits, but Adam desired that she stay home with their firstborn. Early in 2004, a house-hunting trip was planned, which also included Dottie. Neither knew about the training assignment offer by Siemens, but God worked out the details. By the time the child was born, the Gallagher family had moved to their home in Georgia. November 2004 came the news of the training assignment. By January 2005, Dennis was back in a home outside Atlanta with Dottie. The homes in Florida and New York were sold, and life looked wonderful.

A few short months later, everything changed. Dottie had a stomachache. After a large Easter meal two days before, she initially thought it was nothing serious. After it persisted, she went to the doctor, who immediately sent her to the hospital for tests. Dennis was in a training class in Atlanta when she called to tell him the news. A ten-centimeter lump on her liver tested positive for cancer. It had metastasized to her lungs and back. For two years, she received radiation treatments for her back and at least three doses of chemotherapy. By early 2007, the local oncologist had exhausted all options. After searching the Internet, one more out of pocket treatment was available in Houston, Texas. That also was tried without success. By May of 2007, Siemens had allowed working from home and cancelled all training classes for Dennis. Dennis elected to retire, and June 1, 2007 became the date. Dottie passed on that day, which was also the same as Adam and Tricia's anniversary and their daughter, Kelly's birthday.

Throughout the ordeal of battling cancer, God was tugging at Dennis' heart to publish his book, "Legacy of Love." Dennis shrugged it off as something for the family. Signs were everywhere, but Dennis ignored them, until after Dottie's passing. The hole in his heart had to be filled. By the end of the year, "Legacy of Love" was published. Dennis included his wife's story, so you might say it was two legacies. Siemens did not want Dennis to retire and offered a consulting job as a trainer. Ironically, the work he did in May of that year proved to be a successful training course for Siemens. On one trip, Dennis stopped by the training office to pick up some materials. He had a few copies of his book and gave one to a coworker to read. Dennis knew her for eight years and she was unmarried, although her last name was hyphenated. Two weeks later, Dennis showed up at the training center, only to be hugged by this lady. She was all excited. She read the book and then called her ex-husband to read it. The result was a miracle. That two-week period resulted in the couple reuniting and they had remarried. God wanted that book published, if for no other reason, then to reunite two people.

God was watching over Dennis in another way, while Dottie was battling her cancer. After moving to the Atlanta suburb, Dottie enjoyed walking in a local park with her daughter, Tricia. Dottie would prefer to walk daily, but Tricia had a busy schedule conducting homeschool classes. One day the two of them met a small group of ladies, near Dottie's age, walking at the park. They stopped and Tricia asked if her mother could join them on the days, she could not walk. They agreed and a new friendship began. One lady, named Brenda, enjoyed talking with Dottie, and the two of them would find other endeavors to get together. When Dottie learned of her cancer, Brenda felt even closer to her. The two of them met for lunches, enjoyed shopping, and became close friends. Brenda had a heart for people and a love for God. Although Dennis did not meet Brenda until near the end of Dottie's life, he listened to his wife speak so fondly about her.

After several months of friendship, the two of them would face a new hurdle. Brenda had returned from San Francisco with her husband, Benny feeling ill. The news was devastating. Benny had been diagnosed with cancer and it was very advanced. The couple had recently sold their printing business and looked forward to the retirement years. San Francisco may have been part of their plans, but God had other plans. Suddenly, Dottie seemed to be more concerned about her new friend's welfare than her own. Benny died in May of 2006. Dottie fought on for a year and remained close to Brenda.

About a week before Dottie passed, Brenda came over to the house to visit her friend. Dennis was there and it was the first time he remembers meeting her. He was glad to finally put a face to the name and she made a good first impression on him as well. A few weeks after Dottie's death, Brenda felt led to call Dennis. Her words were "I just wanted to say hey. I understand what you are going through." Those were words that were well received. Soon Dennis made the call to invite Brenda to dine with him. Having meals together seemed safe enough. Dennis' daughter, Tricia, told her dad that he should wait for at least a year before seeking a new relationship, as she feared he was vulnerable for a fast rebound. Marriage was not in Brenda's wish list. Dennis found that out rather quickly, but enjoying life together had great healing benefit. Love and friendship remain more than fourteen years later. God helped both through the toughest times.

God also prepared Dottie's best friend, Jan, to be there for her in the last weeks of her life. Jan worked many years as a registered nurse and retired in Florida. The timing could not have been better, as her friend was facing hospice at home in Georgia. Jan felt led to spend, whatever time Dottie had left, with her friend. Her nursing skills were vital as administering morphine or other tasks were daunting to Dennis. It also allowed Dennis to play a round of golf or get out of the house without worry. Someone said that Jan became a nurse, so that someday her skills would be used for her best friend. Perhaps, God allowed that time to help add closure for Jan. There would be no more vacations together as were regularly planned. Family issues were shared daily between them.

Much of those last days were spent with laughter. On one occasion, Dottie was too weak to sit up on the couch, despite heavy pillows wedged on both sides of her. Dottie would start to fall to one side without the strength to stay upright, and shout "oops." Then she would laugh causing the rest in the room to laugh. Tensions were instantly lessened. Perhaps, God was even in the laughter as Dottie was a strong and faithful believer.

God never sleeps. He is always caring for his flock. What a blessing that is.

CHAPTER 16:
DOUGLAS

Doug did not understand much of the situation as the boys grew up. Doug remembers his brothers were always there, even while most other conditions changed. He had a great fear of authority as a child and remembers being a loner at the Harris farm with his fondest memory of having a favorite cow that he would lure to a fence with apples and then climb the fence and hop on the cows back for a ride. Unpleasant memories were of sitting at the table for hours to eat his vegetables – boiled onions. Throwing up proved to be his way out of that unpleasant situation.

When Laverne and Lena were dating and Doug got to visit at Lena's apartment, Doug remembers the happiness of those times and expressed himself in crayon hearts on Lena's walls. When they married, she became mom, not stepmom.

Rarely into athletics, Doug balanced social activities (dances and dates) with studies. His A's and B's were much like his older brothers' achievements. Receiving membership in the National Honor Society, a German society scholarship and a Regents scholarship produced little comment or recognition from Dad. Mom became the voice of what Dad thought and felt, expressing the pride. Dad usually just grunted or nodded. Doug could not seem to talk to Dad.

Like his brothers, Doug worked during his senior year. He enjoyed spending time with his friends and the extra income was essential. One night, after leaving the restaurant, where he was employed, he missed the bus. They ran every half-hour, so he decided to start walking home. The restaurant was in East Irondequoit, while home was over five miles away. He started walking down the road with traffic, as he hoped to catch the next bus. Suddenly, he was sent flying headlong into the gravel. His face was cut from his left ear to well under the chin. The lighting was extremely poor, and the driver did not see him in time.

He was rushed to the nearby hospital, where he was treated. His parents were contacted and came to his side. The number of stitches were too many to count. Doug preferred not to have mom or dad pick him up from work at the late hour as part of his independent spirit. Having them arrive to see him was now more of a relief. The incident could have been much worse, but the hospital was close, and the driver rushed him there without delay.

After the stitches were removed, Doug was referred to a plastic surgeon. Doug remembers that humorously, now. The surgeon told him that if he were a girl it would be a big deal, but to Doug it added personality. When someone asked about how he got his scar, he would tell them to pick the correct answer:

1. He was parachuting and landed in a tree
2. He was in a switch blade gang fight
3. He attempted suicide
4. He failed miserably trying to shave for the first time
5. He was hit by a car

(People rarely picked the correct answer).

Today, Doug looks back at some of the bad things that happened to him, he smiles and remembers the good results. His head took quite a beating over the years. On one occasion, he was swimming in gym class and dove straight down into the shallow end of the pool. By the time he completed the lap, he had along gash on the top of his head and was rushed to the medical department. Today, like his brothers, his forehead has receded dramatically. Those scars look more like a road map. Often God lets us keep our scars as reminders of where we have been and how He has been with us all along.

Doug does not remember a significant event/moment when he came to Christ. Like a great many people, he always felt saved. There is a difference, though, in knowing God exists and knowing God personally. The Bible indicates that everyone knows God exists. It is manifest in each person (Rom 1:19). Those that will come to Christ begin the journey toward knowing God with a small step. For Doug, this step came when the boys lived with their father and Lena on Brayton Road in Greece, a suburb of Rochester, New York. The boys would walk to a little Baptist church on Mt. Read Blvd for Sunday School and church. He remembers that when he was in the 6th grade, he went through a process of asking Jesus to be Lord of his life and confessed his sins with one of the women Sunday school teachers. When he came home and told his parents, all he got was a grunt from his dad and a "That's nice. We don't need to tell everyone though." From Lena. From then on Doug basically kept personal stuff personal and internal.

His faith though was strong. Even when he went to SUNY New Paltz, something was missing until he found a group that went to church and he went with them. It was hard though because their form of religion was different than anything he was used to. A service involved times of people from the congregation standing up and declaring how God did something to them or for them that week. In the army, Doug applied for and almost got a position as a chaplain's assistant. Doug's best friend in Vietnam was Bill Brown, the son of a Baptist minister from Arcade, NY. God was always working behind the scenes to maintain the personal connection with Doug to keep the internal flame alive.

Doug went to SUNY at New Paltz. Math was the only logical major for him. Staying out of the draft was the primary motivation. After 4 years at New Paltz and one semester short of graduation requirements, Doug got drafted in the US Army. Vietnam became his first and only assignment after finishing MP and Correctional Specialist training. Quite a change from the worlds he had known at home and college. Doug worked at "LBJ" (Long Binh Jail), the largest of 2 stockades the army had in Vietnam. He gained respect for security and viewed the experience as a challenge, a learning experience. When discharged, Doug returned home and tried looking for work. Uncle Bob helped, using him as a house painter and handy man. That is how he met Anne. Her family's cottage was just down East Lake Road from Bob and Marion's on Canandaigua Lake.

Doug and Anne were married in Canandaigua on August 11, 1973.

Anne's parents, Anne, Doug, Lena, and Laverne

Uncle Chuck had gotten him a job a Stromberg Carlson as an NC programmer. Even though Doug's real interest had been in the math and computer field, this position grew into engineering augmented by the math that sparked Doug's interest. He pretty much stayed in that and related fields for his career at Stromberg Carlson, then Carter Tool Corporation, then EDS, and finally Siemens.

Joshua Robert was born in 1976 and Marissa Anne in 1978.

Doug, Anne, Joshua, Marissa

By that time, Doug's long-haired look and rock music loving style had settled into a more family man vision. As the years mellowed on him, he began to realize that a lot of the quiet, don't say much but add humor to most things style of dealing with people was how he was and exactly how dad was with him.

Lena's words explaining how dad was and what he felt finally became clear.

In 1991 Doug and Anne left for a winter vacation with their daughter Marissa and son Josh. Josh and his father looked forward to skiing down Whiteface Mountain, while Marissa and Anne would enjoy a shopping trip. The peaks of the Adirondack mountains that came into view may have intensified the four-hour ride. The next morning Anne dropped Doug and Josh off at the mountain to begin their fun day on the slopes. Even though the weather was not cooperating to their hopes and expectations of skiing down slopes used in the Olympics. It had rained the day before but a cold spell this day made a covering of ice everywhere. Looking down the steep slope for their first run must have been breathtaking. What would happen next, surely, changed everything.

Josh led the way with his father right behind. Suddenly, Josh saw one of his father's skis and then his dad slides headfirst past him with no protective headgear. That was near the top of the mountain. After he skied down the trail, he saw a group of ski patrol men at the brick starter gate building and the sound of a helicopter filled the air. That is when he learned that his father had hit the foundation of the building headfirst after sliding down the icy mountain at increasing speeds. Doug was airlifted to the nearest hospital in Plattsburg, New York. Anne was contacted and the family anxiously went to the hospital. Immediately, Anne began contacting her prayer warriors without knowing how severe Doug's condition was.

Upon arriving at the hospital, Anne was notified that Doug suffered massive head trauma and the prognosis was grim. If the swelling on his brain was not contained, he would die. Doug was in a deep coma. The doctors told her that even if he came out of the coma, months of therapy would be necessary to restore the simplest functions like eating or walking. What started out, as a family vacation became a nightmare.

Anne contacted the 700 Club for prayer. She read Bible verses to Doug's as he lay in intensive care in the hospital. She played Christian music to him and continually prayed over him. She maintained close contact with her church family at home for prayer and kept a daily journal that proved valuable for later re-creating these events.

Anne contacted Doug's brothers to let them know what happened. Dennis was the closest and said he would be there the next day. Anne did not know how long the coma would last but welcomed the visitation. Dennis and Dottie arrived the next morning at the hospital. Anne greeted them and said that the swelling had gone down, but Doug was still in the coma. Dennis told her that everything would be all right and Doug would come out of his deep sleep within three days. That may have offered some comfort to Anne, but somehow, she doubted it would happen. On the way there, Dennis lifted his brother in prayer and a peace came over him. He shared that with Anne and said that he believed God was in the restoration business.

The next day, Doug began to show signs of recovery. By the end of the day his eyes opened. His hospital stay would be several days before any form of long-term recovery program would be initiated. Dennis and Dottie went back to Rochester and continued their prayer vigil. Plattsburg did not offer suitable head trauma recovery options, but Saint Mary's Hospital in Rochester did. Transporting Doug there required an ambulance, as the pressure on his brain would not handle air flight. After his extended stay in Plattsburg, Doug recovered well enough to make the trip to Rochester, where he would begin his extensive rehabilitation work. The prognosis indicated that his family would expect months before he would be able to come home. In addition, the likelihood that Doug would be able to go back to work doing computer programming, was near zero.

With his brain functions in question, it was difficult for him to maintain comfort and confidence that that he would be ok. He just had to do what he was told and trust. Initial conferences with doctors prepared Doug and his family for a life where things may change quite drastically. He might need to go for rehabilitation to learn how to do everyday things (like tying his shoes etc.). What happened next was beyond human understanding. Within a few weeks, Doug had regained much of his mental capacity. Slowly, his muscles began to respond to the therapy as well. Dennis made regular visits to assist in his recovery. They would play gin rummy together and initially; Doug would find it difficult to win. Dennis would come and ask if Doug was ready for his therapy, a game of gin. Doug welcomed the time and eventually was able to play competitively.

The doctors kept calling him their miracle patient, especially in the brain injury ward of St. Mary's hospital. Most other brain injury patients would be basically the same day after day. But for Doug, every day something improved, got better. He remembers one of the tests for my brain was to stand on one foot. At first, he just could not do it at all, not for 2 seconds. But then within a few days the nurse would get bored and stop timing after minutes of balance. Day by day he kept improving. Finally, he was released from the hospital. He never needed the rehabilitation.

After about 5 months at home, Doug was able to return to his workplace and performed the tasks required. This was another miracle. On April 5, 1994, the 700-club aired Doug's story with Anne and Doug on the set. There was no denying that God was with them through it all. The ski resort had never used the helicopter rescue prior to that date, which was another miracle. Without that quick response, Doug might not have left the mountain alive through massive blood loss. Another square of God's quilt had been added

Recovery from an accident that, under most circumstances should have taken his life, left a profound impact on Doug. He was left with a "Why me?" feeling. He started asking, "Why did he deserve God's grace? He should have broken my neck." Doug prayed about it and struggled with the answer that he kept getting back – he could not earn anything from God. God just gives grace. That created in him a new awakening to who God is and who He should be in his life. That was the first time that he went from just doing the right things to getting to know God. He joined the Praise and Worship team, jail ministry, and became a Deacon at church. Three times he gave a testimony of the accident and recovery at big church events. God started the process when Doug made a small step toward Him, grew Doug's faith through many experiences, and cemented it with an acceptance of eternal life through grace and not through anything that he could earn. God is still working on him and all of us today.

Ephesians 2:8-10 tells us:

> *"For by grace are ye saved through faith; and not of yourselves: it is the gift of God: Not of works, lest any man should boast. For we are his workmanship, created in Christ Jesus unto good works, which God hath before ordained that we should walk in them."*

CHAPTER 17:
THE QUILT

Grandma Verna and Aunt Effie used to make quilts for all the grandchildren. She did not have a lot of money, but she could gather scraps of cloth that would otherwise be thrown away and then cut and stitch them together to produce a beautiful quilt to warm each child on those cold nights. It was a labor of love. It took a lot of time to choose, cut, and stitch each piece into place. Sometimes it may not be totally clear how it would appear until it was nearly finished. Many of those handmade quilts are now worth a great deal of money. Love changed throwaway scraps to a desirable beautiful tapestry.

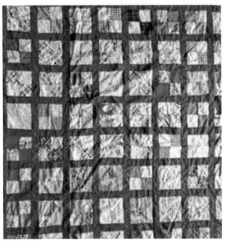

God does the same thing. He is always there. He gathers all the pieces of our lives; the good, the bad, the ugly. When we yield to Him, the Master Quiltmaker then stitches the scraps of our lives into a beautiful quilt, part of the rich tapestry of love for his creation.

And we know that all things work together for good to those who love God, to those who are the called according to His purpose. (Rom 8:28)

This book has been an interesting book to compile. I use the word compile because it is a piecemeal collection of information lived and gathered over many years. Most authors begin a book at the beginning and then proceed systematically to the final chapter. Not so in this case. The first chapter put on paper was chapter 10; even then it was rewritten from a first-person account to the third person. David wanted to know more about his mother and his father and researched all the information he could find on the two of them. Each discovery added another piece of information that he felt should be included. Another scrap for the quilt. Only now after many pieces have been gathered and put in place does the pattern appear. God was there all along. He was guiding the events, nudging each person in the right direction, and even at times protecting them from harm. Laverne and the boys could not see it when they were living through the times. Sometimes they may have even felt God had deserted them or did not care for them. That was never true. God just could see the bigger picture. They could not. They simply needed to trust the LORD. He knows how to put it all together.

Trust in the LORD with all your heart and lean not on your own understanding; in all your ways acknowledge Him and He shall direct your paths. (Prov 3:5,6)

God, however, does not prevent bad things from happening, because to do so would eliminate the consequences of sin. To those who are His or He knows will be His, He will walk with them through the difficulties. He was there when Rex and Verna moved the family to Rochester. If that had not happened, the family would have been in worst straights when Rex fell ill and died of cancer.

Laverne may never have met the love of his life; Rae and their sons may not have been born.

Did angels watch over Laverne as he went off to war? The Bible indicates that those who seek and trust the LORD will have a measure of protection.

How many casualties were prevented by first landing in Africa instead of Normandy to harden the American soldiers first before they had to face the battle-hardened might of the German army. How many bullets and shells were deflected to protect Laverne and his buddies as they lay pinned down at Kesserine pass. Even being captured may ultimately have been a blessing. Did God keep him out of the worst fighting and danger and bring him safely to Tunis where he would be freed by the British. Did God protect him at Normandy first by not putting him and his unit in the first wave on Omaha and the afterwards as they fought their way inland. It will never be known how many bullets and shells may have been deflected from their original targets by angels watching over a man who God knew would eventually accept Christ as His Savior.

> *I will say of the LORD, "He is my refuge and my fortress; my God, in Him I will trust. Surely, He shall deliver you from the snare of the fowler and from perilous pestilence.*
>
> *Because you have made the LORD who is my refuge, even the Most High, your dwelling place, no evil shall befall you, nor shall any plague come near your dwelling; for He shall give His angels charge over you, to keep you in all your ways. (Psa 91:2-3, 9-1)*

Even when Laverne was wounded twice, the wounds were not permanent and would heal. The wounds may have protected him from more serious engagements, but it also brought him home. The first troops to be sent home after the war ended, were the soldiers that had received special medals or purple hearts for their wounds. There was another blessing also. When Laverne was discharged, he was awarded a disability pension particularly for his left arm and shoulder wound. That pension paid him $57.50 per month initially which grew to more than $400 per month by the time of his death.[114] Did God orchestrate the pension so that he would be a little better off during the retirement years?

It was hard when Rae contracted breast cancer. Did God use it, though, to bring her to Christ. Grandma Verna told David many years later that Rae had converted before she died. She and Laverne were married in a Baptist church and may have continued to attend afterwards. Perhaps, both Ray and Laverne made an initial profession of faith during this time. If so, the Apostle Paul's statement in the book of Philippians may well apply.

> *I thank my God upon every remembrance of you, always in every prayer of mine making request for you all with joy, for your fellowship in the gospel from the first day until now being confident of this very thing, that He who has begun a good work in you will complete it until the day of Jesus Christ. (Phil 1:3-6)*

Rae was a strong independent woman. She did well in school, was accepted and graduated from a good university all on her own. Perhaps the cancer brought her face to face with her mortality and her need for a savior. If that is what happened, then David is thanking God for the cancer and looking forward to seeing his mother again in heaven.

When Rae was failing in that back bedroom and took her last look at her boys, she tried to speak but all she could say was I.I.I. David did not understand what his mother was trying to tell him as a 4-year-old boy. He is older now with children and grandchildren. He thinks he knows what she was trying to say. God knew and over the years answered. When the boys needed a mother's love, he provided another mom at least twice. Was it just coincidence that no one was hurt on the destroyer escort Hartley when it was rammed by a tanker and nearly cut in two? Was it just luck that Doug survived being hit by a car and his face dragged on the road with no permanent damage just a scar? Again, was it just luck when Doug was skiing down a mountain

---

114 Taken from discharge medical records and David's personal knowledge of Laverne's income during the last years.

and plowed headfirst into a building without any mental impairment except a few days' memory loss? Some may call it luck, but David passionately believes that God was working behind the scenes to guide and protect. All the boys can point to individual specific answers to prayer. In all those cases, God was answering Rae's unspoken prayer for her boys in the seconds just before her death.

God even tells us that if we look close at the world around us, we will see evidence of Him. If we do not act on what we see, however, and seek Him then He will pour out His wrath on us.

> *For the wrath of God is revealed from heaven against all ungodliness and unrighteousness of men, who suppress the truth in unrighteousness, because what may be known of God is manifest in them, for God has shown it to them. For since the creation of the world His invisible attributes are clearly seen, being understood by the things that are made, even His eternal power and Godhead, so that they are without excuse, because, although they knew God, they did not glorify Him as God, nor were thankful, but became futile in their thoughts, and their foolish hearts were darkened. (Romans 1:18-21)*

If you continue to read the verses after the ones quoted above, you will see what happens to those who do not seek God. Does it not describe our world today? It gets worse.

> *For the wages of sin is death, but the gift of God is eternal life in Christ Jesus our Lord. (Romans 6:23)*

> *For all have sinned and fall short of the glory of God. (Romans 3:23)*

What we deserve for our sin is death and eternal separation from God in a place called hell.

> *But God demonstrates His love toward us, in that while we were still sinners, Christ died for us. (Romans 5:8)*

The gift is not ours, however, until we respond.

> *For God so loved the world that He gave His only begotten Son, that whoever believes in Him should not perish but have everlasting life. (John 3:16)*

The boys, Laverne, and Grandma Verna all knew that God was somewhere out there. They sensed it even if they could not see Him. Each in turn at the right time put their faith in Jesus. They would urge each reader to do the same before it is too late. When we do, He begins stitching the pieces of our lives into a beautiful quilt part of the tapestry of all His children. If we really look close, God might well reveal His handiwork in the very pattern the pieces form together.

EPILOGUE:
PRESENT FAMILIES

David McIntyre Family

Back Row: Stephen Christopher, Sara, Devin, Chris, David, Amy, John, Michelle Middle: Jan, Lisa Front: Harlee, Aiden, Brysin, Gavin

Lisa and Chris

Jeff, Sara, Amy, Harlee

Michelle's mom, John, Michelle, Devin

Dennis McIntyre Family

Dottie

Kelly, Adam, & Tricia   *Bryce*

Jeff, Yvette, Isabella, Felicia, Arielle, Tyler Humphrey

Brenda and Dennis

Douglas McIntyre Family

Back: Megan, Joshua, Amelia, Anne, Marissa, Front: Colin, Doug, Conner

Conner (back)　　　　*Doug, Micah*
Megan, Amelia, Joshua, Colin

Reunion 2022, Doug, David, Dennis

Lightning Source UK Ltd.
Milton Keynes UK
UKHW020720030622
403938UK00006B/85